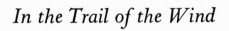

*In the Trail of the Wind*

*Farrar, Straus and Giroux : New York*

# In the Trail of the Wind

*American Indian Poems and Ritual Orations*

*Edited by John Bierhorst*

Acknowledgment is made to the authors and to the University of Oklahoma Press for permission to reprint the following: "Prayer" (Quiché), page 37, from *Popol Vuh: The Sacred Book of the Ancient Quiché Maya* by Delia Goetz and Sylvanus G. Morley, from the Spanish translation by Adrián Recinos, copyright 1950 by the University of Oklahoma Press / "Thus It Is Told" (Aztec), page 6, "To a Woman Loved" (Otomí), page 75, "A Woman's Complaint" (Aztec), page 82, "They Shall Not Wither" (Aztec), page 168, from *Pre-Columbian Literatures of Mexico* by Miguel León-Portilla, copyright 1969 by the University of Oklahoma Press / "Plague" (Cakchiquel), page 150, from *The Annals of the Cakchiquels*, translated by Adrián Recinos and Delia Goetz, copyright 1953 by the University of Oklahoma Press / "Magic Formula against Disease" (Maya), page 151, from *Ritual of the Bacabs*, translated and edited by Ralph L. Roys, copyright 1965 by the University of Oklahoma Press.

Acknowledgment is made to the authors and publishers for permission to reprint from the following (for titles of the selections reprinted, see Notes): "The Symbolic Man of the Osage Tribe" by Francis La Flesche, from *Art and Archaeology*, Vol. IX, February 1920, copyright 1919 by The Archaeological Institute of America / *The Crow Indians* by Robert Lowie, copyright 1935 by Robert Lowie, Holt, Rinehart and Winston, Inc. / *Navajo Creation Myth: The Story of the Emergence* by Hasteen Klah, recorded by Mary C. Wheelwright, with song translations by Harry Hoijer, copyright 1942 Museum of Navaho Ceremonial Art, Inc., Santa Fe, New Mexico / *The Road of Life and Death* by Paul Radin, Bollingen Series V, copyright 1945 by Bollingen Foundation, Princeton University Press / *Songs of the Tewa*, translated by Herbert Joseph Spinden, copyright 1933 by Herbert Joseph Spinden, The Exposition of Indian Tribal Arts, Inc., New York / *Singing for Power* by Ruth Murray Underhill, copyright 1938 by the Regents of the University of California, University of California Press / *Kwakiutl Ethnography* by Franz Boas, edited by Helen Codere, © 1966 by the University of Chicago Press / *Black Elk Speaks* by John G. Neihardt, copyright 1932, 1959 by John G. Neihardt, © 1961 by the University of Nebraska Press.

Acknowledgment is made to the authors and publishers for permission to translate from the following books in Spanish (for titles of the selections translated, see Notes): *Libro de Chilam Balam de Chumayel*, translated from the Maya by Antonio Mediz Bolio, copyright by Antonio Mediz Bolio, Imprenta y Librería Lehmann (Sauter & Co.), San José, Costa Rica / *La Literatura de los Aztecas* by Angel M. Garibay K., © 1964 Editorial Joaquín Mortiz, S.A., Mexico, D.F. / *El Reverso de la Conquista* by Miguel León-Portilla, © 1964 Editorial Joaquín Mortiz, S.A., Mexico, D.F.

# INTRODUCTION

· 1 ·

The ancestors of the American Indian are generally thought to have reached the New World (from northern Asia by way of the Bering Strait) about 12,000 B.C., though some groups may have arrived much earlier and others perhaps as recently as only two thousand years ago. Over long ages successive generations made their way down through Alaska and Canada, eastward to the Atlantic seaboard and southward into Central and South America, until virtually every inhabitable region, including the islands of the Caribbean, had been at least thinly populated.

Many groups continued—and a few in remote regions still continue—to make a livelihood of hunting and gathering. But as early as 5000 B.C. agriculture had begun to take hold, and by 1000 B.C. the cultivation of corn and other crops had become widespread. By A.D. 500 the great cultures of Mexico, Central America, and Peru were already in full flower. (Although these classic civilizations may be taken to represent the pinnacle of Indian achievement, they are by no means superior in every respect. Out of a complex of cultures whose lasting values are not merely technological but especially artistic, even ethical, one may choose to glorify Navajo religion or Kwakiutl painting or Iroquois law as well as, say, Mayan architecture.)

How fragile these cultures were, on one hand, is readily suggested by the history of their submission. In August of 1521 Cortés with merely a few hundred Spanish troops broke the resistance of the Aztecs, forcing the surrender of their last ruler, Cuauhtémoc. Ten years later Pizarro with even fewer men succeeded in capturing the Inca emperor Atahualpa. On both continents populations were decimated by smallpox, tuberculosis, and other alien diseases, often sweeping ahead of the conquerors who had introduced them. By the late nineteenth century the surviving native peoples of North America north of Mexico had been confined to reservations, and the original cultures of the Caribbean had all but vanished through assimilation.

Indian people and Indian life styles have, on the other hand, shown remarkable powers of endurance. In countries like Guatemala, Peru, and Mexico, the native cultures are a permanent fact of national life, notably in Mexico, where an Indianist movement has in recent years brought about what might be termed an Aztec renaissance. In the United States, Indian population has risen steadily since the turn of the century; and while not all tribes have been as successful in maintaining traditional ways as, for instance, the Hopi, a growing emphasis on shared traits promises to elevate once again the cultural prestige, even the political power, of a people that only a few decades ago was thought to be doomed.

· 2 ·

The record of Indian life from prehistoric times to the present, as scantily summarized above, comes to us mainly through the writings of historians and anthropologists. But it can also be traced to a surprising degree in the so-called oral literature—the songs, chants, and speeches—of the people themselves.

If verbal artistry is the essence of literature, then it need not be preserved in writing to be worthy of the name. Even so, much of this oral matter was in fact presented in writing to the outside world. Aztec poetry, Cherokee formulas, and Iroquois ritual oratory, to give a few of the best examples, are known from old manuscripts prepared by Indians, who had learned to write their native languages with either the Roman alphabet or an adaptation of it. Even before contact with European civilization, much Indian literature was handed down through the aid of pictographs (Chippewa), mnemonic beads (Iroquois), or bark-paper books (Maya) elaborately painted with glyphs.

The term "Indian poetry" embraces song-texts primarily; but prayers, incantations, and certain passages from myths, legends, and chronicles may also be included. All of these were transmitted carefully from generation to generation. So were certain fixed speeches used in ritual.

The dividing line between this literature, which is handed down more or less intact, and informal narrative, which varies from mouth to mouth, is hard to draw. Expository or even extemporaneous utterances may also strike the ear as a species of poetry. To show that this is true I have included in the present collection several examples which are neither ritualistic nor strictly poetic, notably the two Aztec omens on pages 138–9 and the two surrender speeches on pages 152–3.

I have included as well a few examples of Eskimo poetry. Eskimos cannot of course be grouped with Indians ethnically, but because they too are a part of the New World their poetry has always been a subject of special interest to students of Indian literature.

The thematic arrangement of the following selections is an attempt to call attention not only to the differences but to the similarities that exist between native American cultures. It should be borne in mind, however, that hundreds of different languages are spoken by American Indians; and needless to say, the indigenous cultures of British Columbia and Guatemala, for example, are very very different. Yet certain aspects of Indian thought seem sufficiently widespread to deserve notice:

*The power of words.* Words are magic, they enable the user to seize control. Sharp coercive phrases like "Listen!" "Be still!" "Drink my blood!" are especially typical of that style of utterance known as the formula. Elsewhere, phrases which seem merely descriptive—for example, "around the roots the water foams" or "my god descended"—may in fact be coercive, uttered in order to *bring about* the action they describe. Much Indian poetry may thus be characterized as compulsive, or incantatory.

*The significance of dreams.* Dreams are thought of as messages from the spirit world, conferring power on the dreamer, who may wish to consolidate this power in a concise symbolic song. Many of the shorter songs in the present collection are dream songs.

*Personality.* Animals and objects, as well as humans, are believed to be imbued with a personifying spirit: for example, deer, water, wind, even hunger or disease. Translators who write *the* deer or *the* wind tend to obscure this quality; but when Frank Russell, translating from the Pima, writes "Wind now commences to sing," the idea is well conveyed.

*Dualism.* Things in nature, colors, even words are thought of in pairs. Indian poetry is replete with paired stanzas and paired expressions: "The white-rising! The yellow-rising!" In many (but not all) cases the idea is evidently an extension of sexuality: white, for example, may be the male color; yellow, the female. The two together make for completeness—not unlike the paired rhyming of English verse, which similarly gives a sense of completeness.

*Father Sky and Mother Earth.* Either the sun or the sky as a whole represents the father figure. Sunlight and rain, descending from the sky, are viewed as life-giving substances that promote fertility within the body of the female earth. (According to some Indian mythologies, human life "emerged" from a womb-like underworld, or series of underworlds, inside the earth.) In some religions (Navajo, for example), the cult of the earth is dominant; in others (Inca), the cult of the sun. In still others the two are worshipped together as a dual creative deity—for example, the Quiché god called "Heart of Heaven, Heart of Earth."

*The cult of the four world quarters.* The four directions (east, west, south, north), corresponding to the four faces of the human body (front, back, left, right), are held sacred in many cultures. By extension, the number 4 itself is also sacred and fourfold repetitions occur frequently in song and myth.

*Anonymity.* The Indian poet does not consider himself the originator of his material but merely the conveyor. Either he has heard it from an elder or he has received it from a supernatural power. Describing more or less the same processes, the self-conscious European or Euro-American poet speaks of reworking traditional materials or, fancifully, of drawing inspiration from a muse. But the Indian, being relatively unself-conscious, does not see it this way. Indian poetry, then, is usually attributed not to an individual but to his culture.

*The influence of alien gods.* In traditional Indian societies, new prayers, new rituals, even new gods are borrowed as readily as new technologies, to be used for whatever good they may bring. Much of Navajo religion was taken from the Pueblos. The Aztecs enshrined countless gods borrowed from tribes they had conquered. Christianity was similarly embraced, but the spirit in which it was taken explains why many "Christianized" Indians are not truly so at all. Christianity has simply been added to a larger body of native custom, which endures.

· 4 ·

The translation of Indian texts presents considerable problems. Aztec and especially old Maya manuscripts can never be interpreted to everybody's satisfaction, and even songs and chants taken directly from the lips of native speakers may be filled with obscurities requiring years of research to illuminate. Translations made before 1850 are generally unreliable—and scarce as well; but in the past hundred years, despite obstacles, a considerable body of tasteful, authoritative translations has accumulated, principally in English but also in Spanish and, to a lesser extent, in German and French. Any list of outstanding contributors would include such names as Washington Matthews (Navajo), James Mooney (Cherokee), Ruth Bunzel (Zuñi), Ralph Roys (Maya), and Angel Garibay (Aztec).

The ideal translation is the lexical, or word-for-word, rendering; but as this rarely yields readable English, the translator resorts to what might properly be called a literal version, in which the words are rearranged with perhaps a few additions and subtractions to make the text comprehensible. A third approach is to completely recast the text in a new mold; thus, the so-called free translation. Still another method should be mentioned: the interpretative translation, in which a skimpy text is filled out with explanatory phrases to convey what the native poet "really meant"—a method now very much out of fashion.

In general, the translations included in this book are literal. Wherever a translation is especially free or, as in a few cases, interpretive, I attempt to make this plain in the notes.

As the sources of Indian poetry are fairly rich, or at least voluminous, it would have been possible to make this anthology somewhat longer. I have deliberately limited it, however, to what I believe to be the best examples of representative types. The book has been conceived not simply as a compendium to be dipped into but rather as a selective progression to be read, one hopes, with a sense of continuity from start to finish.

J. B.

# Contents

## THE ARRIVAL OF THE WHITES

## WE SHALL LIVE AGAIN

# The Beginning

Junction of the Yellowstone and
Missouri Rivers. Painted in 1833 by
Karl Bodmer. This engraving unsigned,
undated (*American History Division,
New York Public Library*)

# THEN HE DESCENDED

Then he descended
while the heavens rubbed against the earth.
They moved among the four lights,
among the four layers of the stars.
The world was not lighted;
there was neither day nor night nor moon.
Then they perceived that the world was being created.
Then creation dawned upon the world.

*Maya*

# SONG OF CREATION

I have made the sun!
  I have made the sun!
Hurling it high
  In the four directions
To the east I threw it
  To run its appointed course.

I have made the moon!
  I have made the moon!
Hurling it high
  In the four directions
To the east I threw it
  To run its appointed course.

*Pima*

# THIS NEWLY CREATED WORLD

Pleasant it looked,
this newly created world.
Along the entire length and breadth
of the earth, our grandmother,
extended the green reflection
of her covering
and the escaping odors
were pleasant to inhale.

*Winnebago*

# THUS IT IS TOLD

Thus it is told, it is said:
there have already been four manifestations
and this one is the fifth age . . .

The first Sun or age which was founded,
its sign was 4-Water,
it was called the Sun of Water.
Then it happened
that water carried away everything.
The people were changed into fish.

Then the second Sun or age was founded.
Its sign was 4-Tiger.
It was called the Sun of Tiger.
Then it happened
that the sky was crushed,
the Sun did not follow its course.
When the Sun arrived at midday,
immediately it was night
and when it became dark,
tigers ate the people . . .

Then the third Sun was founded.
Its sign was 4-Rain-of-Fire.
It happened then that fire rained down,
those who lived there were burned . . .

Its sign was 4-Wind,
when the fourth Sun was founded.
It was called the Sun of Wind.
Then everything was carried away by the wind . . .

The fifth Sun,
4-Movement its sign.
It is called the Sun of Movement . . .
That was when there was light,
when dawn came,
the Sun of Movement which now exists.
4-Movement is its sign.
This is the fifth Sun which was founded,
in it there will be earthquakes,
in it there will be hunger.

*Aztec*

# HE WOVE THE STRANDS OF OUR LIFE

The Flowering Tree stands in Tamoanchan:
There we were created, there he gave us being,
There he wove the strands of our life,
He who gives life to everything.
Likewise I work the gold,
Likewise I polish the jade—it is my song.
It is as if it were turquoise.
For there in Tamoanchan
He turned us round four times,
He who gives life to everything.

*Aztec*

# FIRST MAN WAS
# THE FIRST TO EMERGE

You say there were no people
  Smoke was spreading
You say there were no people
  Smoke was spreading.

First Man was the very first to emerge, they say,
  Smoke was spreading
He brought with him the various robes and precious things, they
    say,
  Smoke was spreading
He brought with him the white corn and the yellow corn, they say,
  Smoke was spreading
He brought with him the various animals and the growing things,
    they say,
  Smoke was spreading.

You say there were no people
  Smoke was spreading.

*Navajo*

# EMERGENCE SONG

Together we emerge with our rattles;
Together we emerge with our rattles,
  Bright-hued feathers in our headdresses.

With our nyññyĭrsa we went down;
With our nyññyĭrsa we went down,
  Wearing Yoku feathers in our headdresses.

This is the White Land; we arrive singing,
  Headdresses waving in the breeze.
We have come! We have come!
  The land trembles with our dancing and singing.

On these black mountains all are singing,
  Headdresses waving, headdresses waving.
We all rejoice! We all rejoice!
  Singing, dancing, the mountains trembling.

*Pima*

# THEY STOOPED OVER AND CAME OUT

Our great fathers talked together. Here they arose and moved
  on. They stooped over and came out from the fourth world,
  carrying their precious things clasped to their breasts.

They stooped over and came out from moss world, carrying
  their precious things clasped to their breasts.
They stooped over and came out from mud world, carrying their
  precious things clasped to their breasts.
They stooped over and came out from wing world, carrying
  their precious things clasped to their breasts.
They stooped over and came out and saw their Sun Father and
  inhaled the sacred breath of the light of day.

*Zuñi*

# UPWARD GOING!

Yonder comes the dawn,
The universe grows green,
The road to the Underworld
Is open! yet now we live,
Upward going, upward going!

*Tewa*

# THE CUSSITAWS COME EAST

At a certain time the Earth opened in the West, where its mouth is. The Earth opened and the Cussitaws came out of its mouth, and settled near by. But the Earth became angry and ate up their children; therefore, they moved farther West. A part of them, however, turned back, and came again to the same place where they had been, and settled there. The greater number remained behind, because they thought it best to do so. Their children, nevertheless, were eaten by the Earth, so that, full of dissatisfaction, they journeyed toward the sunrise.

*Creek*

# OVER THE WATER

The water ran off, the earth dried, the lakes were at rest, all
    was silent . . .

After the rushing waters had subsided the Lenape of the turtle
    were close together, in hollow houses, living together there.

It freezes where they abode, it snows where they abode, it
    storms where they abode, it is cold where they abode.

At this northern place they speak favorably of mild, cool lands,
    with many deer and buffaloes . . .

Over the water, the frozen sea, they went to enjoy it. On the
    wonderful, slippery water, on the stone-hard water all went,

On the great Tidal Sea, the mussel-bearing sea. Ten thousand
    at night, all in one night. To the Snake Island, to the east,
    at night, they walk and walk . . .

Those from the west come with hesitation, esteeming highly
    their old home at the turtle land.

*Delaware*

# NOW WE COME SOUTHWARDS

Long ago in the north
Lies the road of emergence!
Yonder our ancestors live,
Yonder we take our being.

Yet now we come southwards
For cloud flowers blossom here
Here the lightning flashes,
Rain water here is falling!

*Tewa*

# In the Trail of the Wind

Ponca Indians encamped on the banks
of the Missouri. Painted in 1833 by
Karl Bodmer. Engraved *circa* 1850 by
Smillie and Hinshelwood (*Private
collection*)

# IT WAS THE WIND

It was the wind that gave them life. It is the wind that comes out of our mouths now that gives us life. When this ceases to blow we die. In the skin at the tips of our fingers we see the trail of the wind; it shows us where the wind blew when our ancestors were created.

*Navajo*

# BREATHE ON HIM

Breathe on him!
Breathe on him!
Life you alone can give to him.
Long life, we pray, O Father, give unto him!

*Pawnee*

# THE WIND BLOWS FROM THE SEA

By the sandy water I breathe in the odor of the sea,
From there the wind comes and blows over the world,
By the sandy water I breathe in the odor of the sea,
From there the clouds come and rain falls over the world.

*Papago*

# WIND SONG

Wind now commences to sing;
   Wind now commences to sing.
The land stretches before me,
   Before me stretches away.

Wind's house now is thundering.
   Wind's house now is thundering.
I go roaring over the land,
   The land covered with thunder.

Over the windy mountains;
   Over the windy mountains,
Came the myriad-legged wind;
   The wind came running hither.

The black Snake Wind came to me;
   The Black Snake Wind came to me,
Came and wrapped itself about,
   Came here running with its songs.

*Pima*

# THAT WIND

That wind, that wind
Shakes my tepee, shakes my tepee,
And sings a song for me
And sings a song for me.

*Kiowa*

# THE DREAMER RIDES THE WHIRLWIND

Our father, the Whirlwind,
Our father, the Whirlwind—
By its aid I am running swiftly,
By its aid I am running swiftly,
By which means I saw our father,
By which means I saw our father.

*Arapaho*

# BESEECHING THE BREATH

Beseeching the breath of the divine one,
His life-giving breath,
His breath of old age,
His breath of waters,
His breath of seeds,
His breath of riches,
His breath of fecundity,
His breath of power,
His breath of strong spirit,
His breath of all good fortune whatsoever,
Asking for his breath
And into my warm body drawing his breath,
I add to your breath
That happily you may always live.

*Zuñi*

# Give Us Many Good Roads

The Inca presents a libation to the sun.
Designed in 1722 by Bernard Picart
and engraved *circa* 1735 by Claude Du
Bosc (*Picture Collection, New York
Public Library*)

# PRAYER

Creator! you who dwell at the ends of the earth unrivaled, you who gave being and power to men, saying: let this be man, and to women, saying: let this be woman! So saying, you made them, shaped them, gave them being. These you created; watch over them! Let them be safe and well, unharmed, living in peace. Where are you? Up in the sky? Or down below? In clouds? In storms? Hear me, answer me, acknowledge me, give us perpetual life, hold us forever within your hand. Receive this offering wherever you are. Creator!

*Inca*

# PRAYER

Lord most giving and resourceful,
I implore you:
make it your will
that this people enjoy
the goods and riches you naturally give,
that naturally issue from you,
that are pleasing and savory,
that delight and comfort,
though lasting but briefly,
passing away as if in a dream.

*Aztec*

# PRAYER

Greeting, Father's Clansman, I have just made a robe for you, this is it. Give me a good way of living. May I and my people safely reach the next year. May my children increase; when my sons go to war, may they bring horses. When my son goes to war, may he return with black face. When I move, may the wind come to my face, may the buffalo gather toward me. This summer may the plants thrive, may the cherries be plentiful. May the winter be good, may illness not reach me. May I see the new grass of summer, may I see the full-sized leaves when they come. May I see the spring. May I with all my people safely reach it.

*Crow*

# PRAYER

Grandfather, the flowering stick you gave me and the nation's sacred hoop I have given to the people. Hear me, you who have the power to make grow! Guide the people that they may be as blossoms on your holy tree, and make it flourish deep in Mother Earth and make it full of leaves and singing birds.

*Sioux*

# PRAYER

We kneel before you today, Father. We pray you now to forgive us; that our children may not die, but live.

We pray to you for rain, that the fields may be fruitful and that we may have cattle. O Great Gold-Headed Man, and you Great Woman, say, "Let there be rain"; we pray to the two Great Ancient Ones.

May they aid us in all things! May they defend us against harm!

We are gazing upwards; twice will we kneel. O Golden Knife, say, "Let not the children fall sick!"

You are in the midst of heaven. All things were made by you. In you is our life.

*Araucanian*

# PRAYER

Owl!
I have made your sacrifice.
I have prepared a smoke for you.
My feet restore for me.
My legs restore for me.
My body restore for me.
My mind restore for me.
My voice restore for me.
Today take out your spell for me.
Today your spell for me is removed.
Away from me you have taken it.
Far off from me it is taken.
Far off you have done it.
Today I shall recover.
Today for me it is taken off.
Today my interior shall become cool.
My interior feeling cold, I shall go forth.
My interior feeling cold, may I walk.
No longer sore, may I walk.
Impervious to pain, may I walk.
Feeling light within, may I walk.
With lively feelings, may I walk.
Happily may I walk.
Happily abundant dark clouds I desire.
Happily abundant showers I desire.
Happily abundant vegetation I desire.

Happily abundant pollen I desire.
Happily abundant dew I desire.
Happily may I walk.
May it be happy before me.
May it be happy behind me.
May it be happy below me.
May it be happy above me.
With it happy all around me, may I walk.
It is finished in beauty.
It is finished in beauty.

*Navajo*

# PRAYER

Earthmaker, our father, listen to me. On earth, most pitiable is the life we lead. Falling and dying, we stumble along the road. True it is that you told us what to do so that we might obtain the goods and benefits of life. That we are aware of. To achieve the good life as you ordained, this, too, we know and we shall attempt. We shall indeed attempt to secure light and life. But do you, nevertheless, cause real life to appear among us. This is what we ask of you in all humility.

*Winnebago*

# PRAYER

Oh thou, Tzacol, Bitol! Look at us, hear us! Do not leave us, do not forsake us, O God, who art in heaven and on earth, Heart of Heaven, Heart of Earth! Give us our descendants, our succession, as long as the sun shall move and there shall be light. Let it dawn; let the day come! Give us many good roads, flat roads! May the people have peace, much peace, and may they be happy; and give us good life and useful existence!

*Quiché*

# PRAYER

We return thanks to our mother, the earth, which sustains us. We return thanks to the rivers and streams, which supply us with water. We return thanks to all herbs, which furnish medicines for the cure of our diseases. We return thanks to the corn, and to her sisters, the beans and squashes, which give us life. We return thanks to the bushes and trees, which provide us with fruit. We return thanks to the wind, which, moving the air, has banished diseases. We return thanks to the moon and stars, which have given to us their light when the sun was gone. We return thanks to our grandfather *Hé-no,* that he has protected his grandchildren from witches and reptiles, and has given to us his rain. We return thanks to the sun, that he has looked upon the earth with a beneficent eye. Lastly, we return thanks to the Great Spirit, in whom is embodied all goodness, and who directs all things for the good of his children.

*Iroquois*

# WITH REJOICING MOUTH

With rejoicing mouth,
with rejoicing tongue,
by day
and tonight
you will call.
Fasting, you will sing
with the voice of the lark
and perhaps
in our happiness,
in our delight,
from some place in the world,
the creator of man,
the Lord All-powerful,
will hear you.
"Ay!" he will say to you,
and you
wherever you are
and thus forever
with no other lord but him
will live, will be.

*Inca*

# *Home*

Winnebago wigwams. Engraved by
Robert Hinshelwood, after the painting
by Seth Eastman. From Mary Eastman's
*Chicóra,* published in 1854 (*New York
Public Library*)

# AQALÀNI!

But instead of looking south in the direction in which he was
going he looked to the north, the country in which dwelt his
people. Before him were the beautiful peaks of Depentsa, with
their forested slopes. The clouds hung over the mountain, the
showers of rain fell down its sides, and all the country looked
beautiful. And he said to the land, "Aqalàni!" and a feeling of
loneliness and homesickness came over him, and he wept and
sang this song:

> That flowing water! That flowing water!
> My mind wanders across it.
> That broad water! That flowing water!
> My mind wanders across it.
> That old-age water! That flowing water!
> My mind wanders across it.

*Navajo*

# GRANDEUR OF MEXICO

Extended lies the city, lies Mexico, spreading circles of emerald
light, radiating splendor like a quetzal plume.

Beside her the boats of the war chiefs come and go. A flower-
mist spreads out above the people.

O author of life, your house is here! Our father, here you reign!
Your song is heard on earth; it spreads among the people.

Behold Mexico, palace of the white willows, palace of the white
sedges!

And you, like a blue heron, above her you open your wings; you
come to her flying. Beautifully you open your wings and
your fantail.

These are your subjects, they who rule throughout the land,
everywhere!

*Aztec*

# SONG

Mine is a proud village, such as it is,
We are at our best when dancing.

*Makah*

# THE FACE OF MY MOUNTAINS

My voice speaks out
to your lips,
to your face:
give me thirteen times twenty days,
thirteen times twenty nights,
to bid farewell
to the face of my mountains,
the face of my valleys,
where once I roamed
to the four world-ends,
the four world-quarters,
seeking and finding
to feed me
and live.

*Quiché*

# THAT MOUNTAIN FAR AWAY

My home over there, my home over there,
My home over there, now I remember it!
And when I see that mountain far away,
Why, then I weep. Alas! what can I do?
What can I do? Alas! What can I do?
My home over there, now I remember it.

*Tewa*

# HOUSE BLESSING

May it be delightful my house;
From my head may it be delightful;
To my feet may it be delightful;
Where I lie may it be delightful;
All above me may it be delightful;
All around me may it be delightful.

*Navajo*

# THE LANDS AROUND MY DWELLING

The lands around my dwelling
Are more beautiful
From the day
When it is given me to see
Faces I have never seen before.
All is more beautiful,
All is more beautiful,
And life is thankfulness.
These guests of mine
Make my house grand.

*Eskimo*

# The Deer

Hunting deer (southeastern United
States). Painted *circa* 1565 by Jacques
Le Moyne. Engraved *circa* 1590 by
Theodore De Bry (*Picture Collection,
New York Public Library*)

# SONG

Whence does he spring,
the deer?
Whence does he spring,
the deer, the deer, the deer?

*Chippewa*

# BLACK-TAILED DEER SONG

Down from the houses of magic,
  Down from the houses of magic
Blow the winds, and from my antlers
  And my ears they stronger gather.

Over there I ran trembling,
  Over there I ran trembling,
For bows and arrows pursued me.
  Many bows were on my trail.

*Pima*

# SONG OF THE HUNTER

Over there, far off, he runs
With his white forefeet
Through the brush.

Over there, nearby, he runs,
With his nostrils open,
Over the bare ground.

The white tail, climbing,
Seems like a streak on the rocks.
The black tail, striding,
Seems like a crack in the rocks.

*Papago*

# SONG OF THE DEER

Here I come forth.
On the earth I fell over:
The snapping bow made me dizzy.

Here I come forth.
On the mountain I slipped:
The humming arrow made me dizzy.

*Papago*

# SONG OF THE FALLEN DEER

At the time of the White Dawn;
   At the time of the White Dawn,
I arose and went away.
   At Blue Nightfall I went away.

I ate the thornapple leaves
   And the leaves made me dizzy.
I drank the thornapple flowers
   And the drink made me stagger.

The hunter, Bow-Remaining,
   He overtook and killed me,
Cut and threw my horns away.
   The hunter, Reed-Remaining,
He overtook and killed me,
   Cut and threw my feet away.

Now the flies become crazy
   And they drop with flapping wings.
The drunken butterflies sit
   With opening and shutting wings.

*Pima*

# The Words of War

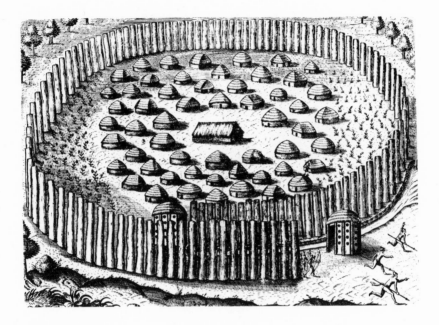

Fortified village (southeastern United
States). Painted *circa* 1565 by Jacques
Le Moyne. Engraved *circa* 1590 by
Theodore De Bry (*Picture Collection,
New York Public Library*)

# WAR SONGS

· 1 ·

From the place of the south
They come,
The birds.
Hear the sound of their passing screams.

· 2 ·

I cast it away,
My body.

· 3 ·

On the front part of the earth,
First strikes the light.
Your power,
Manitou,
Give to me.

*Chippewa*

# WAR SONG

clear the way
in a sacred manner
I come
the earth
is mine

*Sioux*

# SONG OF REPROACH

soldiers
you fled
even the eagle dies

*Sioux*

# SONG OF ENCOURAGEMENT

Within my bowl there lies
Shining dizziness,
Bubbling drunkenness.

There are great whirlwinds
Standing upside down above us.
They lie within my bowl.

A great bear heart,
A great eagle heart,
A great hawk heart,
A great twisting wind—
All these have gathered here
And lie within my bowl.

Now you will drink it.

*Papago*

# HYMN

The nightly drinking, why should I oppose it? Go forth and array yourselves in the golden garments, clothe yourselves in the glittering vestments.

My god descended upon the water, into the beautiful glistening surface; he was as a lovely water cypress, as a beauteous green serpent; now I have left behind me my suffering.

I go forth, I go forth about to destroy, I, Yoatzin; my soul is in the cerulean water; I am seen in the golden water; I shall appear unto mortals; I shall strengthen them for the words of war!

My god appears as a mortal; O Yoatzin, thou art seen upon the mountains; I shall appear unto mortals; I shall strengthen them for the words of war.

*Aztec*

# HOW THE DAYS WILL BE

Indeed, the enemy,
Though in his life
He was a person given to falsehood,
He has become one to foretell
How the world will be,
How the days will be.
That during his time
We may have good days,
Beautiful days,
Hoping for this,
We shall keep his days.
Indeed, if we are lucky,
During the enemy's time
Fine rain caressing the earth,
Heavy rain caressing the earth,
We shall win.
When the enemy's days are in progress,
The enemy's waters
We shall win,
His seeds we shall win,
His riches we shall win,
His power,
His strong spirit,
His long life,
His old age,
In order to win these,

Tirelessly, unwearied,
We shall pass his days.
Now, indeed, the enemy,
Even one who thought himself a man,
In a shower of arrows,
In a shower of war clubs,
With bloody head,
The enemy,
Reaching the end of his life,
Added to the flesh of our earth mother.

*Zuñi*

# THE TAKING OF LIFE BRINGS
## SERIOUS THOUGHTS

We have come thus far, my brothers. We have already laid our
plans. With magic power the trail is made easy, bordered
with flowers, grass, and trees.

The enemy saw the apparent bounty of nature and assembled,
laughing, to gather the seeds and plants. It was the power of
the distant magician which made the enemy enjoy his
fancied prosperity.

In the center of our council ground the fire burned and, lighting
a cigarette, I puffed smoke toward the east. Slowly a vision
arose before me . . .

On the mountain tops was a yellow-spider magician, upon whom
I called for help. He went to the enemy, darkened their
hearts, tied their hands and their bows, and made them
grow weak as women.

Then he pushed us on to destroy the enemy. We rushed upon
the Apaches and killed them without difficulty.

With gladness in my heart I gathered the evidences of my victory
and turned toward home.

You may think this over, my relatives. The taking of life brings
serious thoughts of the waste; the celebration of victory may
become riotous.

*Pima*

## MAGIC FORMULA TO MAKE
## AN ENEMY PEACEFUL

Put your feet down with pollen.
Put your hands down with pollen.
Put your head down with pollen.
Then your feet are pollen;
Your hands are pollen;
Your body is pollen;
Your mind is pollen;
Your voice is pollen.
The trail is beautiful.
Be still.

*Navajo*

# BEHOLD, THIS PIPE

Behold, this pipe. Verily, a man!
Within it I have placed my being.
Place within it your own being, also,
Then free shall you be from all that brings death.

*Osage*

# I PASS THE PIPE

Friend of Wakinyan,
I pass the pipe to you first.
Circling I pass to you who dwell with the Father.
Circling pass to beginning day.
Circling pass to the beautiful one.
Circling I complete the four quarters and the time.
I pass the pipe to the Father with the Sky.
I smoke with the Great Spirit.
Let us have a blue day.

*Sioux*

# Among Flowers That Enclose Us

Marriage ceremony (Panama). Designed
and engraved by Bernard Picart, 1723
(*Picture Collection, New York Public
Library*)

## TO A WOMAN LOVED

In the sky, a moon;
on your face, a mouth.
In the sky, many stars;
On your face, only two eyes.

*Otomí*

# LOVE SONG

New Moon, O New Moon,
Remind that man of me!
Here am I in your presence;
Cause it to be that only I
Shall occupy his heart.

*Tupi*

# LOVE SONG

I know not whether you have been absent:
I lie down with you, I rise up with you,
In my dreams you are with me.
  If my eardrops tremble in my ears,
  I know it is you moving within my heart.

*Nahuatl*

# I CANNOT FORGET YOU

No matter how hard I try to forget you, you always come back
    to my thoughts.
When you hear me singing I am really crying for you.

*Makah*

# MAGIC FORMULA TO FIX
## A BRIDE'S AFFECTION

Listen! Ha! But now you have covered her over with loneliness. Her eyes have faded. Her eyes have come to fasten themselves on one alone. Whither can her soul escape? Let her be sorrowing as she goes along, and not for one night alone. Let her become an aimless wanderer, whose trail may never be followed. O Black Spider, may you hold her soul in your web so that it shall never get through the meshes. What is the name of the soul? They two have come together. It is mine!

*Cherokee*

# LOVE SONG

I go among the girls and see them all,
But I like only the one I walked with first,
My eyes are open for her but I look at the others as though I
    were dreaming,
I say to her, "When I die you must think of me all the time."
I look at the others as though I were dreaming.
The girl is dreaming too.

*Tule*

# SONG OF A CHIEF'S DAUGHTER

Be ready, O chiefs' sons of the tribes! to be my husbands; for I come to make my husband a great chief through my father, for I am mistress, ha ha aya ha ha aya!

I, mistress, come to be your wife, O princes of the chiefs of the tribes! I am seated on coppers, and have many names and privileges that will be given by my father to my future husband, ha ha aya ha ha aya!

For my belt has been woven by my mother, which I use when I look after the dishes that will be given as a marriage present by my father to him who shall be my husband, when many kinds of food shall be given in the marriage feast by my father to him who shall be my husband, ha ha aya ha ha aya!

*Kwakiutl*

# A WOMAN'S COMPLAINT

What shall I do? My man compares me
to a wild red flower.
When I have withered in his hands,
he will leave me.

*Aztec*

# A HUSBAND'S SONG

Dear little wife, dear little wife,
Weep not, cease longing for your home,
Cease longing for your home,
You will be given suet to eat,
Delicious suet,
And eyes, luscious eyes,
All this you will be given.
And tender juicy shoulder pieces
Given you as gifts,
Tender juicy shoulder meat.

*Eskimo*

# LOVE SONG OF A YOUNG MAN

Whenever I eat, I eat the pain of your love, mistress.

Whenever I get sleepy, I dream of my love, my mistress.

Whenever I lie on my back in the house, I lie on the pain of your love, mistress.

For whenever I walk about, I step on the pain of your love, mistress.

*Kwakiutl*

# FRIENDSHIP

Like a quetzal plume, a fragrant flower,
friendship sparkles:
like heron plumes, it weaves itself into finery.
Our song is a bird calling out like a jingle:
how beautiful you make it sound!
Here, among flowers that enclose us,
among flowery boughs you are singing.

*Aztec*

# Of Death

Mandan shrine. Painted in 1833 by
Karl Bodmer. This engraving unsigned,
undated (*American History Division,
New York Public Library*)

# THE BEING WITHOUT A FACE

Our grandfathers, now long dead, and in whom our minds rested in trust, decreed, because they did not know its face, the face, indeed, of that Being that abuses us every day, every night, that Being of Darkness, lying hard by the lodges where it is black night, yea, that Being which here at the very tops of our heads, goes about menacing with its couched weapon—with its uplifted hatchet—eagerly muttering its fell purpose, "I, I will destroy the Work—the Commonwealth," they decreed, I say, that therefore they would call it the Great Destroyer, the Being without a Face, the Being Malefic in Itself, that is Death.

*Iroquois*

# NOT FOREVER ON EARTH

Perchance do we truly live on earth?
Not forever on earth,
But briefly here!
Be it jade, it too will be broken;
Be it gold, it too will be melted,
And even the plume of the quetzal decays.
Not forever on earth,
But briefly here!

*Aztec*

# THE MOON AND THE YEAR

The moon and the year
travel and pass away:
also the day, also the wind.
Also the flesh passes away
to the place of its quietness.

*Maya*

# CHARMS

## · 1 ·

In the spring when we lie down under the young cherry-trees, with the grass green and the sun getting a bit warm, we feel like sleeping, don't we?

## · 2 ·

In the fall when there is a little breeze and we lie in some shelter, hearing the dry weeds rubbing against one another, we generally get drowsy, don't we?

## · 3 ·

In the daytime as the drizzle strikes the lodge pattering and we lie warming the soles of our feet, we fall asleep, don't we?

## · 4 ·

At night when we lie down, listening to the wind rustling through the bleached trees, we know not how we get to sleep but we fall asleep, don't we?

Having looked for a hollow among the thickest pines, we make a fresh camp there. The wind blows on us, and we, rather tired, lie down and keep listening to the rustling pines until we fall asleep.

*Crow*

# SPIRITS

Over the mythical earthlodge above
Spirits are wafted along the roof and drop.
Spirits are wafted and drop down through the doorway.
Flowers bend heavily on their stems.

*Wintu*

# WE SPIRITS DANCE

Down west, down west we dance,
We spirits dance,
We spirits weeping dance.

*Wintu*

# DEATH OF A SISTER

Behold, oh, my sister! you have been deprived of the sight of your bodily self in the light of this day. Verily, as you go from this place and walk along the course of your way, it shall be with a feeling of peace in your heart; so shall it be as you go to Chibiabos. Look not behind you. Strive not to behold your parents and those that are your brothers and sisters. Verily, shall you say to Chibiabos: "This is the message I convey from those whom I have left disconsolate; long life is what they ask of you." You shall say to Chibiabos: "That they may live the full span of life given to man, is what they beg of you."

*Fox*

# WAILING SONG

The sky will weep,
The sky,
At the end of the earth;
The sky will weep.

*Fox*

# MAGIC FORMULA TO DESTROY LIFE

Listen! Now I have come to step over your soul. You are of the wolf clan. Your name is Áyûiuni. Your spittle I have put at rest under the earth.

I have come to cover you over with the black rock. I have come to cover you over with the black cloth. I have come to cover you with the black slabs, never to reappear. Toward the black coffin of the upland in the Darkening Land your paths shall stretch out. So shall it be for you.

The clay of the upland has come to cover you. Instantly the black clay has lodged there where it is at rest at the black houses in the Darkening Land. With the black coffin and the black slabs I have come to cover you.

Now your soul has faded away. It has become blue. When darkness comes your spirit shall grow less and dwindle away, never to reappear. Listen!

*Cherokee*

# DEATH OF A SON

My son, listen once more to the words of your mother. You were brought into life with her pains. You were nourished with her life. She has attempted to be faithful in raising you up. When you were young she loved you as her life. Your presence has been a source of great joy to her. Upon you she depended for support and comfort in her declining days. She had always expected to gain the end of the path of life before you. But you have outstripped her, and gone before her. Our great and wise creator has ordered it thus. By his will I am left to taste more of the miseries of this world. Your friends and relatives have gathered about your body, to look upon you for the last time. They mourn, as with one mind, your departure from among us. We, too, have but a few days more, and our journey shall be ended. We part now, and you are conveyed from our sight. But we shall soon meet again, and shall again look upon each other. Then we shall part no more. Our maker has called you to his home. Thither will we follow. *Na-ho!*

*Iroquois*

# YOU AND I SHALL GO

It is above that you and I shall go;
Along the Milky Way you and I shall go;
Along the flower trail you and I shall go;
Picking flowers on our way you and I shall go.

*Wintu*

# AND YET THE EARTH
# REMAINS UNCHANGED

Ah, flowers that we wear!
Ah, songs that we raise!
—we are on our way to the Realm of Mystery!
If only for one day,
let us be together, my friends!
We must leave our flowers behind us,
we must leave our songs:
and yet the earth remains unchanged.
My friends, enjoy! Friends! Enjoy!

*Aztec*

# Of Rain and Birth

Aztec birth ritual: the male infant
presented with a sword, the female
with a broom. Designed and engraved
by Bernard Picart, 1723 (*Private
collection*)

# SUPPLICATION TO THE RAIN GOD
## AND THE SPIRITS OF WATER

Lord most generous and compassionate,
giver of all sustenance,
Lord, let it be that you comfort the earth
and all those that live on the face of the earth!
Sighing greatly and in anguish,
from my heart I call out;
I implore you, spirits of water,
that lie in the four world-quarters,
the east, the west, the north, the south,
you that dwell in the hollows of the earth,
in the air, in the high peaks, in the deep caves,
to come comfort this poor people,
to water the earth,
for the eyes of those that live on earth
—men, beasts, birds—
are fixed in hope on your persons.
O gods of ours! Let it be that you come!

*Aztec*

# COVER MY EARTH MOTHER

Cover my earth mother four times with many flowers.
Let the heavens be covered with the banked-up clouds.
Let the earth be covered with fog; cover the earth with rains.
Great waters, rains, cover the earth. Lightning cover the earth.
Let thunder be heard over the earth; let thunder be heard;
Let thunder be heard over the six regions of the earth.

*Zuñi*

# IN THE NIGHT

In the night
The rain comes down.
Yonder at the edge of the earth
There is a sound like cracking,
There is a sound like falling.
Down yonder it goes on slowly rumbling.
It goes on shaking.

*Papago*

# OFFERING

That our earth mother may wrap herself
In a fourfold robe of white meal;
That she may be covered with frost flowers;
That yonder on all the mossy mountains
The forests may huddle together with the cold;
That their arms may be broken by the snow,
In order that the land may be thus,
I have made my prayer sticks into living beings.

*Zuñi*

# MY BREATH BECAME

The day broke with slender rain.
The place which is called "lightning's water stands,"
The place which is called "where the dawn strikes,"
Four places where it is called "it dawns with life,"
I land there.
The sky boys, I go among them.
He came to me with long life.
When he talked over my body with the longest life,
The voice of the thunder spoke well four times,
He spoke four times to me with life.
Holy sky youth spoke to me four times.
When he talked to me my breath became.

*Apache*

# BUTTERFLY SONG

Butterfly, butterfly, butterfly, butterfly,
Oh, look, see it hovering among the flowers,
It is like a baby trying to walk and not knowing how to go.
The clouds sprinkle down the rain.

*Acoma*

# SONGS OF BIRDS

## · 1 ·

In time of rain I come:
I can sing among the flowers:
I utter my song: my heart is glad.

## · 2 ·

Water of flowers foams over the earth:
My heart was intoxicated.

*Aztec*

## WORDS SPOKEN BY A MOTHER
## TO HER NEWBORN SON
## AS SHE CUTS THE UMBILICAL CORD

I cut from your middle the naval string: know you, understand that your birthplace is not your home, for you are a server and a warrior, you are the bird called quechol, you are the bird called zacuan, you are the bird and warrior of the One Who Dwells in All Places. This house where you are born is but a nest. It is a way station to which you have come. It is your point of entrance into this world. Here you sprout, here you flower. Here you are severed from your mother, as the chip is struck from the stone.

*Aztec*

# PRESENTING AN INFANT TO THE SUN

Now this is the day.
Our child,
Into the daylight
You will go out standing.
Preparing for your day,
We have passed our days.
When all your days were at an end,
When eight days were past,
Our sun father
Went in to sit down at his sacred place.
And our night fathers
Having come out standing to their sacred place,
Passing a blessed night
We came today.
Now this day
Our fathers,
Dawn priests,
Have come out standing to their sacred place.
Our sun father,
Having come out standing to his sacred place,
Our child, it is your day.
This day,
The flesh of the white corn,
Prayer meal,
To our sun father
This prayer meal we offer.

May your road be fulfilled
Reaching to the road of your sun father,
When your road is fulfilled
In your thoughts may we live,
May we be the ones whom your thoughts will embrace,
For this, on this day
To our sun father,
We offer prayer meal.
To this end:
May you help us all to finish our roads.

*Zuñi*

# SONGS IN THE GARDEN
# OF THE HOUSE GOD

· 1 ·

The sacred blue corn-seed I am planting,
In one night it will grow and flourish,
In one night the corn increases,
In the garden of the House God.

The sacred white corn-seed I am planting,
In one day it will grow and ripen,
In one day the corn increases,
In its beauty it increases.

· 2 ·

With this it grows, with this it grows,
The dark cloud, with this it grows.
The dew thereof, with this it grows,
The blue corn, with this it grows.

With this it grows, with this it grows,
The dark mist, with this it grows.
The dew thereof, with this it grows,
The white corn, with this it grows.

## · 3 ·

This it eats, this it eats,
The dark cloud,
Its dew
The blue corn eats,
This it eats.

This it eats, this it eats,
The dark mist,
Its dew
The white corn eats,
This it eats.

## · 4 ·

The great corn-plant is with the bean,
Its rootlets now are with the bean,
Its leaf-tips now are with the bean,
Its dewdrops now are with the bean,
Its tassel now is with the bean,
Its pollen now is with the bean,
And now its silk is with the bean,
And now its grain is with the bean.

Truly in the East
The white bean
And the great corn-plant
Are tied with the white lightning.
Listen! It approaches!
The voice of the bluebird is heard.

Truly in the East
The white bean
And the great squash
Are tied with the rainbow.
Listen! It approaches!
The voice of the bluebird is heard.

From the top of the great corn-plant the water gurgles, I hear it;
Around the roots the water foams, I hear it;
Around the roots of the plants it foams, I hear it;
From their tops the water foams, I hear it.

The corn grows up. The waters of the dark clouds drop, drop.
The rain descends. The waters from the corn leaves drop, drop.
The rain descends. The waters from the plants drop, drop.
The corn grows up. The waters of the dark mists drop, drop.

Since the ancient days, I have planted,
Since the time of the emergence, I have planted,
The great corn-plant, I have planted,
Its roots, I have planted,
The tips of its leaves, I have planted,
Its dew, I have planted,
Its tassel, I have planted,
Its pollen, I have planted,
Its silk, I have planted,
Its seed, I have planted.

Since the ancient days, I have planted,
Since the time of the emergence, I have planted,
The great squash-vine, I have planted,
Its seed, I have planted,
Its silk, I have planted,
Its pollen, I have planted,
Its tassel, I have planted,
Its dew, I have planted,
The tips of its leaves, I have planted,
Its roots, I have planted.

Shall I cull this fruit
Of the great corn-plant?
Shall you break it? Shall I break it?
Shall I break it? Shall you break it?
      Shall I? Shall you?

Shall I cull this fruit
Of the great squash-vine?
Shall you pick it up? Shall I pick it up?
Shall I pick it up? Shall you pick it up?
      Shall I? Shall you?

*Navajo*

# Dreams

Eskimo kayak (northwestern Greenland).
Unattributed engraving published in
Elisha Kent Kane's *U.S. Grinnell
Expedition*, 1854 (*Picture Collection,
New York Public Library*)

# SONG

My mother bore me,
    Ah!
Within a raincloud,
    Ah!
That I might weep with the rain,
    Ah!
That I might whirl with the cloud,
    Ah!

*Quechua*

# THE GREAT SEA

The great sea
Has sent me adrift,
It moves me as the weed in a great river,
Earth and the great weather
Move me,
Have carried me away
And move my inward parts with joy.

*Eskimo*

# DREAM SONG

Above the place where the minnow maiden sleeps while her fins
    move gently in the water,
Flowers droop,
Flowers rise back again.

*Wintu*

# DREAM SONG

as my eyes
search
the prairie
I feel the summer
in the spring

*Chippewa*

# THE SONG OF A DREAM

Now, my friends, please hear:
it is the song of a dream:
each spring the gold young corn
gives us life;
the ripened corn gives us refreshment;
to know that the hearts of our friends
are true is to put around us
a necklace of precious stones.

*Aztec*

# AT NIGHT MAY I ROAM

at night may I roam
against the winds may I roam
at night may I roam
when the owl is hooting
may I roam

at dawn may I roam
against the winds may I roam
at dawn may I roam
when the crow is calling
may I roam

*Sioux*

# DREAM SONG

Where the mountain crosses.
On top of the mountain, I do not myself know where.
I wandered where my mind and my heart seemed to be lost.
I wandered away.

*Papago*

# DREAM SONG

Sometimes
I go about pitying myself
While I am carried by the wind
Across the sky

*Chippewa*

# IS THIS REAL

Let us see, is this real,
Let us see, is this real,
This life I am living?
You, Gods, who dwell everywhere,
Let us see, is this real,
This life I am living?

*Pawnee*

# IN THE GREAT NIGHT

In the great night my heart will go out,
Toward me the darkness comes rattling,
In the great night my heart will go out.

*Papago*

# DREAM SONG

Where will you and I sleep?
At the down-turned jagged rim of the sky you and I will sleep.

*Wintu*

# Omens and Prophecies

"The Last of Their Race." Engraved *circa* 1850 by Rice and Buttre, after the painting by T. B. Matteson (*American History Division, New York Public Library*)

# SONG

The sweet-voiced quechol there, ruling the earth, has intoxicated my soul.

I am like the quetzal bird, I am created in the house of the one and only God; I sing sweet songs among the flowers; I chant songs and rejoice in my heart.

The fuming dewdrops from the flowers in the field intoxicate my soul.

I grieve to myself that ever this dwelling on earth should end.

I foresaw, being a Mexican, that our rule began to be destroyed, I went forth weeping that it was to bow down and be destroyed.

Let me not be angry that the grandeur of Mexico is to be destroyed.

The smoking stars gather together against it; the one who cares for flowers is about to be destroyed.

He who cared for books wept, he wept for the beginning of the destruction.

*Aztec*

# OMEN

By daylight a fire fell. Three stars together it seemed: flaming, bearing tails. Out of the west it came, falling in a rain of sparks, running to east. The people saw, and screamed with a noise like the shaking of bells.

*Aztec*

# OMEN

By night a voice was heard in the air: a woman, crying, "Oh, my children, we must go far away." At times she cried: "Oh, my children, where can I take you?"

*Aztec*

# PROPHECY

Many winters ago, our wise ancestors predicted that a great monster, with white eyes, would come from the east and, as he advanced, would consume the land. This monster is the white race, and the prediction is near its fulfillment. They advised their children, when they became weak, to plant a tree with four roots, branching to the north, the south, the east, and the west; and then collecting under its shade, to dwell together in unity and harmony. This tree, I propose, shall be this very spot. Here we will gather, here live, and here die.

*Iroquois*

# PROPHECY

Eat, eat, thou hast bread;
Drink, drink, thou hast water;
On that day, dust possesses the earth,
On that day, a blight is on the face of the earth,
On that day, a cloud rises,
On that day, a mountain rises,
On that day, a strong man seizes the land,
On that day, things fall to ruin,
On that day, the tender leaf is destroyed,
On that day, the dying eyes are closed,
On that day, three signs are on the tree,
On that day, three generations hang there,
On that day, the battle flag is raised,
And they are scattered afar in the forests.

*Maya*

# The Arrival of the Whites

Encounter (United States, eastern
seaboard). Designed by Alfred R. Waud
and engraved by Charles H. Smith
*circa* 1860 (*American History Division,
New York Public Library*)

# WHO ARE THEY?

A great land and a wide land was the east land,
A land without snakes, a rich land, a pleasant land.
Great Fighter was chief, toward the north.
At the Straight river, River-Loving was chief.
Becoming-Fat was chief at Sassafras land . . .

Affable was chief, and made peace with all,
All were friends, all were united under this great chief.
Great-Beaver was chief, remaining in Sassafras land.
White-Body was chief on the seashore.
Peace-Maker was chief, friendly to all.
He-Makes-Mistakes was chief, hurriedly coming . . .

Coming-as-a-Friend was chief; he went to the Great Lakes,
Visiting all his children, all his friends.
Cranberry-Eater was chief, friend of the Ottawas.
North-Walker was chief; he made festivals.
Slow-Gatherer was chief at the shore . . .

White-Crab was chief; a friend of the shore.
Watcher was chief; he looked toward the sea.
At this time, from north and south, the whites came.
They are peaceful; they have great things; who are they?

*Delaware*

# I GAVE THEM FRUITS

· 1 ·

My children, when at first I liked the whites,
My children, when at first I liked the whites,
I gave them fruits,
I gave them fruits.


· 2 ·

Father, have pity on me,
Father, have pity on me;
I am crying for thirst,
I am crying for thirst;
All is gone—I have nothing to eat,
All is gone—I have nothing to eat.

*Arapaho*

# THE WEEPING SPREADS

The weeping spreads,
In Tlatelolco the tears are dripping.
The Mexicans have taken flight across the water;
They are like women; everyone flees.
"Where are we going? Oh, my friends!"
Then: "Was it true?"
Yes, already the city of Mexico is abandoned;
The smoke rises; the haze spreads.

*Aztec*

# THEY CAME FROM THE EAST

They came from the east when they arrived.
Then Christianity also began.
The fulfillment of its prophecy is ascribed to the east . . .
Then with the true God, the true *Dios*,
came the beginning of our misery.
It was the beginning of tribute,
the beginning of church dues,
the beginning of strife with purse-snatching,
the beginning of strife with blow-guns,
the beginning of strife by trampling on people,
the beginning of robbery with violence,
the beginning of forced debts,
the beginning of debts enforced by false testimony,
the beginning of individual strife,
a beginning of vexation.

*Maya*

# THE BEGINNING OF SICKNESS

Then they adhered to their reason.
There was no sin;
in the holy faith their lives were passed.
There was then no sickness;
they had then no aching bones;
they had then no high fever;
they had then no smallpox;
they had then no burning chest;
they had then no abdominal pains;
they had then no consumption;
they had then no headache.
At that time the course of humanity was orderly.
The foreigners made it otherwise when they arrived here.
They brought shameful things when they came . . .
this was the cause of our sickness also.
There were no more lucky days for us;
we had no sound judgment.
At the end of our loss of vision,
and of our shame,
everything shall be revealed.

*Maya*

# PLAGUE

Great was the stench of the dead. After our fathers and grand-fathers succumbed, half of the people fled to the fields. The dogs and the vultures devoured the bodies. The mortality was terrible. Your grandfathers died, and with them died the son of the king and his brothers and kinsmen. So it was that we became orphans, O my sons! So we became when we were young. All of us were thus. We were born to die!

*Cakchiquel*

# MAGIC FORMULA AGAINST DISEASE

Curses on the snake of creation,
the snake of darkness,
the unique enemy of man,
the unique enemy of Anom,
when he was awakened!
Behead him, scratch him,
ye gods in the earth,
ye gods in the heavens!
Let there be an end to his career!
Let there be an end to the advantage
of the lust of creation,
the lust of darkness . . .
Ye gods in the earth!
Slap ye him;
clasp ye him violently,
the lust of creation,
the lust of darkness.
He is directly to be cut off,
mostly his pain, mostly his fever . . .
Curses upon him!
Cut ye his outer covering.
Scratch it off!

*Maya*

# THE SURRENDER SPEECH OF
# CUAUHTÉMOC

Ah, captain, I have done everything within my power to defend my kingdom and deliver it from your hands. But as fortune has not favored me, take my life; it will be most fitting; and in so doing you will bring an end to the Mexican kingdom, for already you have ruined and destroyed my city and my people.

*Aztec*

# THE SURRENDER SPEECH OF
## CHIEF JOSEPH

I am tired of fighting. Our chiefs are killed. Looking Glass is dead. Toohulhulsote is dead. The old men are all dead. It is the young men who say yes or no. He who led the young men is dead. It is cold and we have no blankets. The little children are freezing to death. My people, some of them, have run away to the hills and have no blankets, no food. No one knows where they are—perhaps freezing to death. I want to have time to look for my children and see how many of them I can find. Maybe I shall find them among the dead. Hear me, my chiefs, I am tired. My heart is sick and sad. From where the sun now stands I will fight no more forever.

*Nez Percé*

# ON THE DEATH OF ATAHUALPA

We weep,
tears of blood,
we weep,
In despair, crying,
we weep;
the sun forever has stolen
the light from his eyes.
No more his face do we see,
no more his voice do we hear,
nor will his affectionate gaze
watch over his people.

*Quechua*

# THE GHOST OF CAUPOLICÁN

Who is this,
like the tiger,
riding the wind
with his phantom-like body?
When the oaks see him,
when the people see him,
they speak with hushed voices,
saying one to another:
"Lo, brother, there is
the ghost of Caupolicán."

*Araucanian*

# CURSE ON PEOPLE THAT WISH ONE ILL

Suwa! Segaltimaya! May you speak to make me happy! May you suddenly experience that wherewith you curse me! May you suddenly fall dead without being sick! May you fall dead, you who drink my blood! May you suddenly all perish! Drink my blood! Would that I might be happy! May I not be sick in any way!

*Yana*

# WE ARE LIVING HUMBLY

· 1 ·

We are living humbly on this earth,
We are living humbly on this earth,
We are living humbly on this earth,
We are living humbly on this earth,
We are living humbly on this earth.
Our Heavenly Father, we want everlasting life through Jesus
    Christ.
We are living humbly on this earth.

· 2 ·

When I die I will be at the door of heaven and
Jesus will take me in.

*Cheyenne*

# We Shall Live Again

Buffalo and elk, upper Missouri River.
Painted in 1833 by Karl Bodmer.
Unattributed engraving published in
Thomas Addison Richards' *Romance
of American Landscape*, 1854 (*Picture
Collection, New York Public Library*)

# AT THE WOOD'S EDGE

Now today I have been greatly startled by your voice coming through the forest to this opening. You have come with troubled mind through all obstacles. You kept seeing the places where they met on whom we depended, my offspring. How then can your mind be at ease?

You kept seeing the footmarks of our forefathers; and all but perceptible is the smoke where they used to smoke the pipe together. Can then your mind be at ease when you are weeping on your way?

Great thanks now, therefore, that you have safely arrived. Now, then, let us smoke the pipe together. Because all around are hostile agencies which are each thinking, "I will frustrate their purpose." Here thorny ways, and here falling trees, and here wild beasts lying in ambush. Either by these you might have perished, my offspring, or by the uplifted hatchet in the dark outside the house. Every day these are wasting us; or deadly invisible disease might have destroyed you, my offspring.

Great thanks now, therefore, that in safety you have come through the forest.

*Iroquois*

# REQUICKENING

Now do we pass our hands through your tears in sympathy; now,
we wipe away the tears from your face, using the white
fawn-skin of pity.

Now, therefore, let them say, we have wiped away your tears.

Now, therefore, in peace of mind, you will continue to look
around yourself, enjoying again the light of the day. Now,
also, you will again behold what is taking place on the earth,
whereon is outspread the handiwork of the Master of All
Things.

Now, also, you will again see your nephews and nieces, as they
move about your person, even to the least of them, the in-
fants. Now, you will see them all again.

Now, therefore, verily, you will again do your thinking in peace,
you, my offspring, noble one, you whom I have held in my
bosom.

*Iroquois*

# MAGIC FORMULA

You have no right to trouble me,
Depart, I am becoming stronger;
You are now departing from me,
You who would devour me;
I am becoming stronger, stronger.
Mighty medicine is now within me,
You cannot now subdue me—
I am becoming stronger,
I am stronger, stronger, stronger.

*Iroquois*

# SONG

And I think over again
My small adventures
When with a shore wind I drifted out
In my kayak
And thought I was in danger.
My fears,
Those I thought so big,
For all the vital things
I had to get and to reach.

And yet, there is only
One great thing,
The only thing:
To live to see in huts and on journeys
The great day that dawns,
And the light that fills the world.

*Eskimo*

# THE DAY HAS RISEN

The day has risen,
Go I to behold the dawn,
Hao! you maidens!
Go behold the dawn!
The white-rising!
The yellow-rising!
It has become light.

*Hopi*

# THERE!

There!
There!
Beautiful white-rising has dawned.
Beautiful yellow-rising has dawned.
There!
There!

*Hopi*

# COME ALL!

Come all! Stand up!
Just over there the dawn is coming.
Now I hear
Soft laughter.

*Papago*

# THEY SHALL NOT WITHER

They shall not wither, my flowers,
They shall not cease, my songs.
I, the singer, lift them up.
They are scattered, they spread about.
Even though on earth my flowers
may wither and yellow,
they will be carried there,
to the innermost house
of the bird with the golden feathers.

*Aztec*

# THEY WILL APPEAR

They will appear—may you behold them!
They will appear—may you behold them!
A horse nation will appear.
A thunder-being nation will appear.
They will appear, behold!
They will appear, behold!

*Sioux*

# YOU SHALL LIVE

A thunder-being nation I am, I have said.
A thunder-being nation I am, I have said.
You shall live.
You shall live.
You shall live.
You shall live.

*Sioux*

# SONG OF THE GHOST DANCE

The crow
I saw him when he flew down
To the earth
He has renewed our life
He has taken pity on us

*Cheyenne*

# SONGS OF THE GHOST DANCE

### · 1 ·

The wind stirs the willows
The wind stirs the willows
The wind stirs the grasses
The wind stirs the grasses

### · 2 ·

Fog! Fog!
Lightning! Lightning!
Whirlwind! Whirlwind!

### · 3 ·

The whirlwind!
The whirlwind!
The snowy earth comes gliding,
The snowy earth comes gliding.

· 4 ·

There is dust from the whirlwind.
There is dust from the whirlwind.
The whirlwind on the mountain,
The whirlwind on the mountain.

· 5 ·

The rocks are ringing,
The rocks are ringing.
They are ringing in the mountains,
They are ringing in the mountains.

*Paiute*

# SONGS OF THE GHOST DANCE

· 1 ·

The sun's beams are running out
The sun's beams are running out
The sun's yellow rays are running out
The sun's yellow rays are running out

· 2 ·

We shall live again
We shall live again

*Comanche*

# The Beginning

PAGE 3 / Translated from the Maya by Ralph Roys, in his *The Book of Chilam Balam of Chumayel,* 1933, p. 101. *He*: Ah Uuc Cheknal, a fertility god. *The heavens rubbed against the earth*: a recurring Indian idea, suggesting the primeval mating of Father Sky and Mother Earth. (Ah Uuc Cheknal is to be identified with the sky.) *They moved:* Indian origin myths are seldom creation stories in the strict sense; there is usually a preexisting "they" moving about who witness or participate in the creation. *There was neither day . . .* : an echo of Genesis 1:2. (See Introduction, under "The influence of alien gods.")

PAGE 4 / Translated from the Pima by Frank Russell, in his "The Pima Indians," *Bureau of American Ethnology, 26th Annual Report, 1904–05,* pp. 207–8. Earth Magician, the Pima Creator, threw the sun to the north sky, but it would not run its proper course; then to the west sky; then to the south sky. Finally he threw it to the east, and it rose. Likewise the moon.

PAGE 5 / Translated from the Winnebago by Paul Radin, in his *The Road of Life and Death,* 1945, p. 254. Though the composition is Indian, there are probably ideas from Genesis in this as in the two preceding selections from the Maya and from the Pima. The remaining selections in this book are, I believe, free of missionary influence, except where otherwise noted.

PAGES 6–7 / Translated from the Aztec by Miguel León-Portilla, in his *Pre-Columbian Literatures of Mexico* (copyright 1969 by the University of Oklahoma Press), pp. 35–7. The Aztecs believed there had been four previous worlds, or "suns," each of which had been destroyed. *4-Water, 4-Tiger, 4-Rain-of-Fire, 4-Wind, 4-Movement*: These are dates, like Friday the 13th; each "sun," or world, is named after the day on which it was or will be destroyed. (The Sun of Water was destroyed by water on the day 4-Water; the Sun of Movement, which is our present world, will be destroyed by "movement" i.e., earthquake, on the day 4-Movement; etc.) *Tigers*: jaguars (or ocelots?). *That was when there was light, when dawn came*: One might assume there had been light during the previous "suns," but Aztec mythology treats the coming of dawn as a separate, unconnected event.

PAGE 8 / Translated from the Aztec by Angel Garibay, in his *La Literatura de los Aztecas*, 1964, p. 55. (The English version is mine, after the Spanish of Garibay.) *Flowering Tree*: symbolic source of life. (Compare the Sioux prayer on p. 32 and the Iroquois prophecy on p. 140.) *Tamoanchan*: the Aztec paradise. *He*: the Creator. *Gold, jade*: standard Aztec metaphors for song.

PAGE 9 / Translated from the Navajo by Harry Hoijer, in Hasteen Klah's *Navajo Creation Myth*, 1942, p. 135. First Man and his companions emerged into the Fifth—the present—World from the Fourth World. (Beneath the Fourth World are three earlier worlds, all within the earth.) *You say there were no people*: an ironic taunt directed to the listener (probably a young person) who doubts the teaching. *Smoke was spreading*: smoke from the fires of men?—evidently an affirmation of the existence of people and hence of the correctness of the doctrine. *Precious things*: hard goods (e.g., jewelry, pottery) as opposed to soft goods (here translated "various robes").

PAGE 10 / Translated from the Pima by Frank Russell, in his "The Pima Indians," *Bureau of American Ethnology, 26th Annual Report, 1904–05*, p. 226. *Nyñnyĭrsa, Yoku*: archaic words whose meanings are lost. *We went down*: These mythic people were not actually created in the underworld; they entered the earth and were subsequently reborn. *White*: color associated with sunlight? *We arrive*: we emerge—i.e., we are born (or, more precisely, reborn).

PAGE 11 / Translated from the Zuñi by M. C. Stevenson, in her "The Zuñi Indians," *Bureau of American Ethnology, 23rd Annual Report, 1901–02*, p. 77. *Precious things*: fetishes to bring rain and crops. *Moss world*: the

Third World. *Mud world:* the Second World. *Wing world:* the First World, where sunlight was first glimpsed. (Sunbeams are called wings; they were seen penetrating through the opening in the earth.) Compare note to p. 9 above.

PAGE 12 / Translated from the Tewa by Herbert J. Spinden, in his *Songs of the Tewa,* 1933, p. 93.

PAGE 13 / Translated from the Creek by A. S. Gatschet, in his *A Migration Legend of the Creek Indians,* 1888, p. 9. *Cussitaw:* name of a Creek band. *The Earth . . . ate up their children:* possibly a reference to disease, thought to be borne by foul gases rising from marshes. (Thus, according to Gatschet, they believed the earth was angry with them.)

PAGE 14 / Translated from the Delaware by D. G. Brinton, in his *The Lênapé and Their Legends,* 1885, pp. 181ff. These lines are from the *Walam Olum,* the migration legend of the Delawares (who call themselves Lenape, meaning "people"; they also refer to themselves as turtle men). Some see in this passage a specific reference to migration from Asia via the Bering Strait! Brinton's more plausible theory places the remembered ancestral land in Labrador; and the "frozen" or "great tidal" sea is the St. Lawrence River. It must be conceded that Brinton's translation of this extremely difficult and archaic text is based heavily on guesswork. *The water ran off:* i.e., after the primeval flood. Such a flood occurs in countless mythologies the world over, including, of course, the Christian.

PAGE 15 / Translated from the Tewa by Herbert J. Spinden, in his *Songs of the Tewa,* 1933, p. 97.

## In the Trail of the Wind

PAGE 19 / Translated from the Navajo by Washington Matthews, in his *Navaho Legends,* 1897, p. 69. *Them:* First Man and First Woman—the Navajo Adam and Eve—to whom the wind imparted the breath of life. *The trail of the wind:* an allusion to the circular motion of the whirlwind, which appears to have left its imprint in the more or less circular skin whorls at the tips of human fingers.

PAGE 20 / Translated from the Pawnee by Alice Fletcher, in her "The Hako," *Bureau of American Ethnology, 22nd Annual Report, 1900-01*, Part 2, p. 361. *Him*: the infant for whom this song of blessing is sung. The translation is interpretive, and I have revised it slightly.

PAGE 21 / Translated from the Papago, in Frances Densmore's "Papago Music," *Bureau of American Ethnology, Bulletin 90, 1929*, p. 173. The English version of this song is apparently a revision by Densmore of the translation made for her by her interpreter, whom she does not specifically identify.

PAGE 22 / Translated from the Pima by Frank Russell, in his "The Pima Indians," *Bureau of American Ethnology, 26th Annual Report, 1904-05*, p. 324. A "medicine song"—sung to effect a cure.

PAGES 23-4 / Translated from the Kiowa, and from the Arapaho, by James Mooney, in his "The Ghost Dance Religion," *Bureau of American Ethnology, 14th Annual Report, 1892-93*, Part 2, pp. 1087, 970. These are both songs of the Ghost Dance. See note to pp. 172-4.

PAGE 25 / Translated from the Zuñi by Ruth Bunzel, in her "Zuñi Ritual Poetry," *Bureau of American Ethnology, 47th Annual Report, 1929-30*, p. 701. One line omitted.

## Give Us Many Good Roads

PAGE 29 / Translated from the old Quechua by Cristóbal de Molina, in his *Relación de las Fábulas y Ritos de los Incas* (ed. H. H. Urteaga), 1916, p. 47. Recorded about 1575. The English version is mine, after the Spanish of Molina.

PAGE 30 / Freely translated from the Aztec by Bernardino de Sahagún, in his *Historia General de las Cosas de Nueva España*, Libro 6, capítulo 2. (The English version is mine, after the Spanish of Sahagún.) Sahagún's great *Historia* contains thirteen "books," compiled in the 1500's, detailing the cultural life of pre-conquest Mexico. In facing columns he recorded the testimony obtained from the lips of Indians (copied down for him in the Aztec language by native scribes) and his own, rather free, Spanish translation. The Spanish, available in several editions, has never been fully published in English. An English version of the Aztec (except Book 6) is published as *Florentine Codex*, translated by C. A. Dibble and A. Anderson.

PAGE 31 / Translated from the Crow by Robert Lowie, in his *The Crow Indians*, 1935, p. 115. *Father's Clansman*: a term of respect, here used as an address to the sun. *A robe*: of white buffalo hide, an offering to the sun. *Black face*: symbol of victory. (A warrior who slays an enemy blackens his face.) *May the wind come to my face*: so that game will not scent me.

PAGE 32 / Translated from the Sioux by Benjamin Black Elk (son of Black Elk) and revised by John G. Neihardt, in Neihardt's *Black Elk Speaks*, 1932, pp. 176–7. Specifically, the hoop stands for the Sioux camp, which is a circle of tepees; in a general way it symbolizes the life of the Sioux nation. The source of that life is the flowering tree, thought of as growing in the center of the hoop.

PAGE 33 / Translated from the Araucanian, in Agustín Edwards' *Peoples of Old*, 1929, p. 39. (Edwards does not identify the translator of this prayer.) *We kneel . . . we pray . . . forgive us*: apparent Christianisms; but it is worth noting that the confession of sins was practiced in America long before the coming of the whites. *Great Gold-Headed Man*: the sun? *Great Woman*: the earth? *Golden Knife*: the sun??

PAGES 34–5 / Translated from the Navajo by Washington Matthews, in his *The Night Chant*, 1902, p. 73. *Sacrifice*: an offering of pollen, jewels, and a ritual cigarette, all contained in a corn husk. *It is finished in beauty*: Matthews likens this standard Navajo prayer closing to the Christian amen.

PAGE 36 / Translated from the Winnebago by Paul Radin, in his *The Road of Life and Death*, 1945, p. 123.

PAGE 37 / Translated from the old Quiché, in *Popol Vuh: The Sacred Book of the Ancient Quiché Maya*, by Delia Goetz and Sylvanus Morley, from the Spanish translation by Adrián Recinos (copyright 1950 by the University of Oklahoma Press), p. 173. *Tzacol, Bitol*: the double name of the Creator, translated "Creator, Maker."

PAGE 38 / Translated from the Iroquois by Ely S. Parker, in Lewis Morgan's *League of the Ho-de-no-sau-nee*, 1851, pp. 202–3. *Hé-no*: tutelary of rain and thunder. (As thunderer he has the power to strike witches, snakes, and evildoers generally.) Note in this prayer the progression from earth to sky. The final sentence suggests Christian influence.

PAGE 39 / Translated from the old Quechua by José María Arguedas, in his *Poesía y Prosa Quechua*, 1967, p. 22. This Inca hymn, sung for the benefit of newly elected priests, was recorded in Quechua about 1613 by Juan de Santa Cruz Pachacuti. The English version is mine, after the Spanish of Arguedas.

## Home

PAGE 43 / Translated from the Navajo by Washington Matthews, in his "The Mountain Chant," *Bureau of American Ethnology, 5th Annual Report, 1883–84*, p. 393. *Aqalàni*: Greeting! *Depentsa*: name of some mountain or group of mountains in southern Colorado (La Plata Mts.?), home of the young man who is the subject of these lines. *That flowing water*: the San Juan River. (The young man has crossed the river and is looking back.) *Old-age*: Matthews' idea was probably that the water conveys the blessing of long life; that is, the ability to reach old age.

PAGE 44 / Translated from the Aztec by Angel Garibay, in his *La Literatura de los Aztecas*, 1964, p. 71. (The English version is mine, after the Spanish of Garibay.) The ancient city of Mexico was built on low marshy islands in the middle of an extensive lake (now drained); hence the references to boats, willows, and sedges. Exquisite birds such as the green-plumed quetzal and the "blue heron" were held sacred, considered in some cases to be the embodiment of divine powers. This typical song is addressed to the war god, protector of Mexico.

PAGE 45 / Translated from the Makah, in Frances Densmore's "Nootka and Quileute Music," *Bureau of American Ethnology, Bulletin 124*, 1939, p. 81. The English version of this song is apparently a revision by Densmore of the translation made for her by her interpreter, Hazel Parker Butler.

PAGE 46 / From *Teatro Indígena Prehispánico* (Prólogo de Francisco Monterde), 1955, pp. 88-9. (The unattributed Spanish version presented by Monterde is probably based not on the Quiché text directly but on the French translations of Brasseur and Raynaud; the English version is mine, after the Spanish in Monterde.) In these lines from the ancient Quiché drama, *Rabinal Achí*, a prisoner pleads with his captor. *Thirteen times twenty days*: 260 days is the Quiché religious year; the prisoner's request might be freely translated "Give me a year."

PAGE 47 / Translated from the Tewa by Herbert J. Spinden, in his *Songs of the Tewa*, 1933, p. 72.

PAGE 48 / Translated from the Navajo by Cosmo Mindeleff, in his "Navaho Houses," *Bureau of American Ethnology, 17th Annual Report, 1895-96* (published 1898), p. 505.

PAGE 49 / Translated from the Eskimo by Knud Rasmussen, in his *Intellectual Culture of the Iglulik Eskimos* (translated from Rasmussen's Danish into English by W. E. Calvert), 1930, p. 27. The Iglulik live along the northwest shore of Hudson Bay.

## The Deer

PAGE 53 / Translated from the Chippewa by Frances Densmore, in her

"Chippewa Music II," *Bureau of American Ethnology, Bulletin 53*, 1913, p. 201. In this typical Chippewa dream song the singer envisions a deer dancing.

PAGE 54 / Translated from the Pima by Frank Russell, in his "The Pima Indians," *Bureau of American Ethnology, 26th Annual Report, 1904–05*, p. 317. *Houses of magic*: The Southwest abounds in ruins of ancient Pueblo dwellings, thought by later Indians to be the houses of gods.

PAGES 55–6 / Translated from the Papago by Ruth Underhill, in her *Singing for Power*, 1938, pp. 58–9.

PAGE 57 / Translated from the Pima by Frank Russell, in his "The Pima Indians," *Bureau of American Ethnology, 26th Annual Report, 1904–05*, pp. 299–300.

## The Words of War

PAGE 61 / Translated from the Chippewa by H. R. Schoolcraft, in his *Oneóta*, 1845, p. 347. (I have revised Schoolcraft's translation somewhat.) *They come, the birds*: The bird referred to may be a predator, which the warrior emulates; or it may be the loon, which was thought by the Chippewa to be an omen of victory in war. In the second song the warrior expresses eagerness for a glorious death in battle. In the third he addresses the sun. Manitou, often translated "god," is a name that can be applied to any super-natural power—in this case, the sun.

PAGES 62–3 / Translated from the Sioux by Frances Densmore (with the assistance of Robert P. Higheagle), in her "Teton Sioux Music," *Bureau of American Ethnology, Bulletin 61*, 1918, pp. 351, 394. *In a sacred manner*: i.e., painted with war paint.

PAGE 64 / Translated from the Papago by Ruth Underhill, in her *Singing for Power*, 1938, p. 97. An elder guardian presents a bowl of water to a young warrior after a ritual fast. In his song the guardian suggests images which may come to the warrior in his dreams and serve as omens of victory in battle.

PAGE 65 / Translated from the Aztec by D. G. Brinton, in his *Rig Veda Americanus*, 1890, p. 57. One of the finest and most famous of Indian poems. Brinton was the first to render it in a modern language; and although later scholars have found serious errors in many of Brinton's pioneering translations, this one remains substantially valid. Consider the hymn as a dialogue between the priest and the god (or a priest impersonating the god). The first stanza is sung by the god, the second by the priest, the third by the god, and the fourth by the priest. The god is Xipe Totec (shee-pay toe-tek, the flayed one, here called Yoatzin), a god of fertility whose needs must be satisfied by war—in the following manner: human victims are taken on the battlefield and handed over to priests, who flay them; the skins of the victims are then worn by the priests as ritual garments ("the glittering vestments"), symbolizing the renewal of vegetation, or the putting on of new life. *The nightly drinking*: The ritual is performed at night by priests who deliberately make themselves drunk. (Like the use of tobacco, the use of alcohol or of narcotics is sacred in many Indian cultures.)

PAGES 66-7 / Translated from the Zuñi by Ruth Bunzel, in her "Zuñi Ritual Poetry," *Bureau of American Ethnology, 47th Annual Report, 1929-30*, p. 680. These lines are spoken over the scalp of the enemy as part of a ritual spanning several days. *He has become one to foretell*: It is expected that the scalp will cause an omen of good fortune. *We shall keep his days*: i.e., we shall observe the several days' ritual, which is spoken of as the "enemy's time," or the "enemy's days," or simply "his time."

PAGE 68 / Translated from the Pima by Frank Russell, in his "The Pima Indians," *Bureau of American Ethnology, 26th Annual Report, 1904-05*, pp. 363-5. A somewhat interpretive translation, made with the assistance of native speakers. *Cigarette*: The cigarette is, of course, an invention of the American Indian. Formerly it consisted of native tobacco, often mixed with other herbs, enclosed in a reed or similar vegetable material. The mild euphoria induced by the inhalation of tobacco smoke might help to put one in touch with a supernatural power—in this case the yellow-spider magician.

PAGE 69 / Translated from the Navajo by Washington Matthews, in his *Navaho Legends*, 1897, p. 109. *Pollen*: the most sacred material used in Navajo ritual, frequently sprinkled as a benediction. Here it symbolizes peace.

PAGE 70 / Translated from the Osage by Francis La Flesche, in *Art and Archaeology*, Feb. 1920, p. 72. From the Osage war rite, a ceremony to insure success in battle. The pipe, smoked as an offering to supernatural powers, is here considered as a symbolic man, representing the unity of the tribe. The translation is interpretive.

PAGE 71 / Translated from the Sioux by J. R. Walker, in *Anthropological Papers of the American Museum of Natural History*, Vol. 16, Part 2, 1917, p. 157. A medicine man's invocation to the winds, asking for fair skies and propitious circumstances. *Friend of Wakinyan*: the West Wind. (Wakinyan is a mythological being who dwells in the west with the West Wind and hence is his friend.) *You who dwell with the Father*: the North Wind. (The reference is to a mythological episode.) *Beginning day*: east, the direction of sunrise (figuratively, the East Wind). *The beautiful one*: female companion to the South Wind (an indirect way of addressing the South Wind). *Circling I complete . . . the time*: The medicine man who recited these lines provided the following explanation: "The circle is the symbol of time, for the daytime, the nighttime, and the moon time are circles above the world, and the year time is a circle around the border of the world." *The Father*: the original and supreme Wind, father of the four winds, who ordinarily dwells directly above, i.e., "with the sky."

## Among Flowers That Enclose Us

PAGE 75 / Translated from the Otomí by Angel Garibay, in his *Historia de la Literatura Náhuatl*, I, p. 239. The English version is by Miguel León-Portilla, after the Spanish of Garibay, from León-Portilla's *Pre-Columbian*

*Literatures of Mexico* (copyright 1969 by the University of Oklahoma Press), p. 95.

PAGE 76 / Translated from the Tupi by J. V. Couto de Magalhães, in his *O Selvagem*, 1876, p. 142. The English version is by Herbert J. Spinden, after the Portuguese of Couto, from Spinden's *Songs of the Tewa*, 1933, p. 37.

PAGE 77 / Translated from the Nahuatl, in D. G. Brinton's *Essays of an Americanist*, 1890, p. 295. Brinton notes that this song was collected in Mexico by Karl Hermann Berendt, but he does not say who made the translation. I have made slight revisions in the version given by Brinton.

PAGE 78 / Translated from the Makah, in Frances Densmore's "Nootka and Quileute Music," *Bureau of American Ethnology, Bulletin 124*, 1939, p. 328. (The English version of this song is apparently a revision by Densmore of the translation made for her by her interpreter, Hazel Parker Butler.) This Makah song and the one preceding, from the Nahuatl, both suggest the influence of European sentimentality.

PAGE 79 / Translated from the Cherokee by James Mooney, in his "The Sacred Formulas of the Cherokees," *Bureau of American Ethnology, 7th Annual Report, 1885–86*, p. 383. This formula, or "prayer," spoken by a young bridegroom, is addressed to the Black Spider. *What is the name of the soul?*: The bride's soul is thought of as a person in its own right; by learning its name, the bridegroom would gain power over it.

PAGE 80 / Translated from the Tule, in Frances Densmore's "Music of the Tule Indians of Panama," *Smithsonian Miscellaneous Collections*, Vol. 77, No. 11, 1926, p. 34. (The English version of this song is apparently a revision by Densmore of the translation made for her by her interpreter, Alfred Robinson.) European sentimentality is obvious here.

PAGE 81 / Translated from the Kwakiutl by Franz Boas, in his "Ethnology of the Kwakiutl," *Bureau of American Ethnology, 35th Annual Report,*

*1913–14*, Part 2, p. 1314. *Coppers*: pieces of copper given away in a boastful display of wealth.

PAGE 82 / Translated from the Aztec by Miguel León-Portilla, in his *Pre-Columbian Literatures of Mexico* (copyright 1969 by the University of Oklahoma Press), pp. 114–15.

PAGE 83 / Translated from the Eskimo by Knud Rasmussen, in his *Intellectual Culture of the Iglulik Eskimos* (translated from Rasmussen's Danish into English by W. E. Calvert), 1930, p. 153. The Iglulik live along the northwest shore of Hudson Bay.

PAGE 84 / Translated from the Kwakiutl by Franz Boas, in his *Kwakiutl Ethnography* (ed. Helen Codere), 1966, p. 348.

PAGE 85 / Translated from the Aztec by Angel Garibay, in his *La Literatura de los Aztecas*, 1964, p. 51. (The English version is mine, after the Spanish of Garibay.) *Quetzal*: a tropical American bird, prized for its brilliant green plumage. *Jingle*: The Aztec copper jingle is similar to the European sleigh bell.

## Of Death

PAGE 89 / Translated from the Iroquois by J. N. B. Hewitt (ed. W. Fenton), in *Journal of the Washington Academy of Sciences*, Mar. 15, 1944, p. 75. *Commonwealth*: the League of the Iroquois.

PAGE 90 / Translated from the Aztec by Angel Garibay, in his *Poesía Náhuatl*, II, 1965, pp. 3–4. (The English version is mine, after the Spanish of Garibay.) Song attributed to Nezahualcoyotl, fifteenth-century poet-king of Texcoco (a city-state allied with the Aztec capital of Mexico).

PAGE 91 / Freely translated from the Maya by Antonio Mediz Bolio, in his *El Libro de Chilam Balam de Chumayel*, 1930, p. 35. (The English version is mine, freely based on the Spanish of Mediz.) These lines (in the Spanish of Mediz) are inscribed over the doorway to the Mayan collections at the Museum of Anthropology, Mexico City.

PAGES 92–3 / Translated from the Crow by Robert Lowie, in his *The Crow Indians*, 1935, pp. 109–10. The speaker, who wishes to strike a death blow without fear of struggle, uses these charms to bring sleep upon his enemy.

PAGES 94–5 / Translated from the Wintu by D. Demetracopoulou, in his "Wintu Songs," *Anthropos*, Vol. 30, 1935, p. 487.

PAGE 96 / Translated from the Fox by William Jones, in *Publications of the American Ethnological Society*, Vol. 1, 1907, p. 383. Not merely a lamentation, but an expression of fear (of the ghost) and a plea for intercession with Chibiabos (chi-BYE-a-bohs), ruler of the land of the dead.

PAGE 97 / Translated from the Fox by Truman Michelson, in his "The Owl Sacred Pack of the Fox Indians," *Bureau of American Ethnology, Bulletin 72*, 1921, p. 29.

PAGE 98 / Translated from the Cherokee by James Mooney, in his "The Sacred Formulas of the Cherokees," *Bureau of American Ethnology, 7th Annual Report, 1885–86*, p. 391. *Wolf, Áyûiuni*: Typical Cherokee clan name and personal name. The user of this formula substitutes the clan and personal names of his victim.

PAGE 99 / Translated from the Iroquois by Ely S. Parker, in Lewis Morgan's *League of the Ho-de-no-sau-nee*, 1851, pp. 175–6. (I have made slight revisions in the translation given by Morgan.) *Na-ho*: "I have finished," or "So be it."

PAGE 100 / Translated from the Wintu by D. Demetracopoulou, in his "Wintu Songs," *Anthropos*, Vol. 30, 1935, p. 485.

PAGE 101 / Translated from the Aztec by Angel Garibay, in his *La Literatura de los Aztecas*, 1964, p. 57. The English version is mine, after the Spanish of Garibay.

# Of Rain and Birth

PAGE 105 / Freely translated from the Aztec by Bernardino de Sahagún, in his *Historia General de las Cosas de Nueva España*, Libro 6, capítulo 8. (The English version is mine, after the Spanish of Sahagún.) See note to p. 30. *Lord*: Tlaloc, the rain god.

PAGE 106 / Translated from the Zuñi by M. C. Stevenson, in her "The Zuñi Indians," *Bureau of American Ethnology, 23rd Annual Report, 1901–02*, p. 176. *The six regions of the earth*: the four world quarters (see Introduction) plus the zenith and the nadir—a stylized way of saying "everywhere," or "throughout the world."

PAGE 107 / Translated from the Papago by Ruth Underhill, in her *Singing for Power*, 1938, p. 154.

PAGE 108 / Translated from the Zuñi by Ruth Bunzel, in her "Introduction to Zuñi Ceremonialism," *Bureau of American Ethnology, 47th Annual Report, 1929–30*, pp. 483–4. *I have made my prayer sticks into living beings*: The prayer stick is an effigy. Were this an Aztec prayer, the sacrifice would literally be human; here it is figurative. (Human sacrifice is rare north of Mexico.)

PAGE 109 / Translated from the Apache by Pliny Goddard, in *Holmes Anniversary Volume*, 1916, pp. 134–5. *He came to me*: sky boy, or sky youth, a supernatural being whose power is here invoked. In the preceding line he is pluralized as "sky boys"; Indian speakers frequently use the plural form in addressing a deity or supernatural power. (It is perhaps worth noting that while English speakers do not use the terms "god" and "gods" interchangeably, Christians nonetheless think of God as three persons in one.)

PAGE 110 / Translated from the Keresan, in Frances Densmore's "Music of Acoma, Isleta, Cochiti and Zuñi Pueblos," *Bureau of American Ethnology, Bulletin 165*, 1957, p. 38. (The English version of this song is apparently a revision by Densmore of the translation made for her by her interpreter, whom she does not identify.) Keresan is the language of Acoma.

PAGE 111 / Translated from the Aztec by Angel Garibay, in his *La Literatura de los Aztecas*, 1964, pp. 84-5. The English version is mine, after the Spanish of Garibay.

PAGE 112 / Freely translated from the Aztec by Bernardino de Sahagún, in his *Historia General de las Cosas de Nueva España*, Libro 6, capítulo 31. (The English version is mine, after the Spanish of Sahagún.) See note to p. 30. *Quechol, zacuan*: sacred birds, believed to harbor the souls of slain warriors. The mother here promises her son the glorious death of a warrior. (The warrior's duty is to obtain victims for sacrifice. Compare the hymn on p. 65, and note the illustration on p. 103.)

PAGES 113-14 / Translated from the Zuñi by Ruth Bunzel, in her "Zuñi Ritual Poetry," *Bureau of American Ethnology, 47th Annual Report, 1929-30*, pp. 635-6. The Zuñi child is presented to the sun on the tenth day of his life. *When eight days were past*: reference is to the ninth day of the infant's life, the day before the sunrise ceremony in which this prayer is used. *Our sun father went in to sit down at his sacred place*: sunset (of the ninth day). *Night fathers*: the night itself, personified and pluralized. (See note to p. 109). *Dawn priests*: dawn itself; the reference here is to dawn of the tenth day, the day of the ceremony. *Our sun father, having come out standing to his sacred place*: i.e., daybreak. *White corn, prayer meal*: White meal, emblem of (male) human flesh, is offered to the sun. If the child were female, yellow meal would be offered.

PAGES 115-19 / Translated from the Navajo by Washington Matthews, in *Journal of American Folklore*, Vol. 7, 1894, pp. 187-93. A sequence of songs to promote growth. According to myth, they were originally sung by the god Hastshéhogan (translated House God by Matthews). All the songs have two stanzas (I have omitted the second stanza in a few cases), the second of which is mainly an artistic device, a verbal echo of the first. (See Introduction, under "Dualism.") In song no. 8, note the reference to the Emergence.

(Compare the poems on pp. 9, 10, and 11.) In song no. 5, the line "Listen! It approaches!" refers to the rain; bluebird is a Navajo symbol for joy.

## *Dreams*

PAGE 123 / Translated from the Quechua by R. and M. d'Harcourt, in their *La Musique des Incas*, 1925, p. 368. The English version is mine, after the French of the d'Harcourts.

PAGE 124 / Translated from the Eskimo by Knud Rasmussen, in his *Intellectual Culture of the Iglulik Eskimos* (translated from Rasmussen's Danish into English by W. E. Calvert), 1930, p. 123.

PAGE 125 / Translated from the Wintu by D. Demetracopoulou, in his "Wintu Songs," *Anthropos*, Vol. 30, 1935, p. 485.

PAGE 126 / Translated from the Chippewa by Frances Densmore, in her "Chippewa Music II," *Bureau of American Ethnology, Bulletin 53*, 1913, p. 254.

PAGE 127 / Translated from the Aztec by Angel Garibay, in his *Poesía Náhuatl*, II, 1965, p. 121. The English version is mine, after the Spanish of Garibay.

PAGE 128 / Translated from the Sioux by Frances Densmore (with the assistance of Robert P. Higheagle), in her "Teton Sioux Music," *Bureau of American Ethnology, Bulletin 61*, 1918, p. 186. Observe the dualistic form as pointed out above in note to pp. 115–19.

PAGE 129 / Translated from the Papago, in Frances Densmore's "Papago Music," *Bureau of American Ethnology, Bulletin 90*, 1929, p. 206. The English version of this song is apparently a revision by Densmore of the translation made for her by her interpreter, whom she does not specifically identify.

PAGE 130 / Translated from the Chippewa by Frances Densmore, in her "Chippewa Music," *Bureau of American Ethnology, Bulletin 45,* 1910, p. 127.

PAGE 131 / Translated from the Pawnee, in D. G. Brinton's *Essays of an Americanist,* 1890, p. 292.

PAGE 132 / Translated from the Papago, in Frances Densmore's "Papago Music," *Bureau of American Ethnology, Bulletin 90,* 1929, p. 126. The English version of this song is apparently a revision by Densmore of the translation made for her by her interpreter, whom she does not specifically identify.

PAGE 133 / Translated from the Wintu by D. Demetracopoulou, in his "Wintu Songs," *Anthropos,* Vol. 30, 1935, p. 485.

## Omens and Prophecies

PAGE 137 / Translated from the Aztec by D. G. Brinton, in his *Ancient Nahuatl Poetry,* 1887, p. 123. This well loved translation by Brinton is almost certainly erroneous. (The original Aztec text from which it derives is evidently a war song, as shown by Garibay in his *Poesía Náhuatl,* III, p. 12.) I include it as a romantic curio to be compared with the genuine omens (see below), with which Brinton was undoubtedly familiar.

PAGE 138–9 / Translated from the Aztec by Bernardino de Sahagún, in his *Historia General de las Cosas de Nueva España,* Libro 12, capítulo 1. The English versions are mine, based on the Spanish of Sahagún and compared with several modern translations made directly from the Aztec. See note to p. 30.

PAGE 140 / Translated from the Iroquois by Ely S. Parker, in Lewis Morgan's League of the *Ho-de-no-sau-nee,* 1851, p. 277.

PAGE 141 / Translated from the Maya by D. G. Brinton, in his *The*

*Maya Chronicles*, 1882, p. 127. One of Brinton's best translations. The interesting resemblance to Ecclesiastes 12:1–7 is coincidental.

## The Arrival of the Whites

PAGE 145 / Translated from the Delaware by D. G. Brinton, in his *The Lênapé and Their Legends*, 1885, pp. 207ff. These excerpts, chronicling the succession of Delaware chiefs down to the arrival of the whites, are from the last part of the *Walum Olum*. (See note to p. 14.) *They are peaceful; they have great things; who are they?*: the final line of the *Walam Olum*; "things" is a reference to ships.

PAGE 146 / Translated from the Arapaho by James Mooney, in his "The Ghost Dance Religion," *Bureau of American Ethnology, 14th Annual Report, 1892-93*, Part 2, pp. 961, 977.

PAGE 147 / Translated from the Aztec by Miguel León-Portilla, in his *El Reverso de la Conquista*, 1964, p. 62. (The English version is mine, after the Spanish of León-Portilla.) *Tlatelolco*: a section of the ancient city of Mexico. Compare the song on p. 44.

PAGE 148 / Translated from the Maya by Ralph Roys, in his *The Book of Chilam Balam of Chumayel*, 1933, pp. 77–9. *Dios*: the Spanish word for God. There is evidently no irony intended in the phrase "true God"; the Indians accepted the Christian *Dios*—though not the cruelty and hypocrisy that went with it.

PAGE 149 / Translated from the Maya by Ralph Roys, in his *The Book of Chilam Balam of Chumayel*, 1933, p. 83. *In the holy faith*: a reference to the Christian-like virtue (so viewed in retrospect) of pre-conquest days. If there is an element of shame in this passage, it is that—in the confusion of the conquest—excesses were committed not only by whites but by Indians against their own kind.

PAGE 150 / Translated from the Cakchiquel by Adrián Recinos (with Delia

Goetz), in his *The Annals of the Cakchiquels* (copyright 1953 by the University of Oklahoma Press), p. 116. This passage describing the horrors of disease borne by the conquistadors appears to have been written in the form of an ancient song. The plague was probably smallpox.

PAGE 151 / Translated from the Maya by Ralph Roys, in his *Ritual of the Bacabs* (copyright 1965 by the University of Oklahoma Press), pp. 46–7; and in his *The Book of Chilam Balam of Chumayel*, 1933, p. 99, footnotes 3, 4. This is merely a sampling of a much longer formula, uttered by a shaman (medicine man) for the benefit of his patient. Note that the disease is personified and that the shaman's verbal assault is directed against the father and the mother of the disease as well as the disease itself. The following symbols are used: snake = the disease; creation = the male deity who fathered the disease; darkness = the female deity who mated with "creation" to produce the disease. *Anom*: the first man to be created, or "awakened," i.e., the Maya Adam. (The gods in the earth and in the heavens are deities whose aid is here invoked.)

PAGE 152 / Translated from the Aztec by Ramírez of Otumba, in Fernando de Alva Ixtlilxochitl's *Obras Históricas*, 1891, p. 378. (The English version is mine, after the Spanish of Ramírez.) Cuauhtémoc, the last Aztec ruler, surrendered to Cortés in August of 1521.

PAGE 153 / Translated from the Nez Percé by Arthur Chapman, in Herbert J. Spinden's "The Nez Percé Indians," *Memoirs of the American Anthropological Association*, Vol. II, Part 3, 1908, p. 243. (See also Alvin M. Josephy's *The Nez Percé Indians and the Opening of the Northwest*, 1965, p. 630.) Chief Joseph surrendered to the U. S. Army in October of 1877. *Looking Glass, Toohulhulsote*: names of chiefs serving with Joseph.

PAGE 154 / Translated from the Quechua by D. Alomías Robles, in Jorge Basadre's *Literatura Inca*, 1938, p. 105. (The English version is mine, after the Spanish of Alomías.) The Inca Atahualpa was executed by Pizarro in August of 1533. But this Quechua song, tinged with European sentimentality, dates from the nineteenth century.

PAGE 155 / Translated from the Araucanian by Tomás Guevara, in his *Folklore Araucano*, 1911, p. 133. (The English version, after the Spanish of Guevara, is that of Agustín Edwards in his *Peoples of Old*. I have slightly revised Edwards' translation.) The famous Araucanian chief, Caupolicán, was tortured and killed by Spanish troops in 1558. But this song evidently dates from the nineteenth century.

PAGE 156 / Translated from the Yana by Edward Sapir, in *University of California Publications in American Archaeology and Ethnology*, Vol. 9, No. 1, 1910, p. 199. (I have made a few small revisions in Sapir's translation.) *Suwa*: word used in Yana formulas, something like "abracadabra." *Segaltimaya*: meaning unclear, perhaps an address to supernatural powers. *Drink my blood*: A better translation might be "Drink-me my blood," or, freely, "Let *me* drink blood!" ("To drink blood" is to cast a curse.)

PAGE 157 / From Frances Densmore, *American Anthropologist*, Vol. 43, No. 1, 1941, pp. 81, 82. Two songs of the Native American Church, a modern Indian religion based on Christianity. Densmore does not identify her translator, and though it appears that she found these songs among the Cheyenne it is not in fact clear whether she found them among the Cheyenne or the Winnebago, or both.

## We Shall Live Again

PAGE 161 / Translated from the Iroquois by Horatio Hale, in his *The Iroquois Book of Rites*, 1883, pp. 117–18. Part of a speech in which the three "elder" nations (the Mohawk, the Onondaga, and the Seneca) address the two "younger" nations (the Oneida and the Cayuga). Thus the speaker uses the form "my offspring." The "younger" nations, having made their way through the forest from their home villages, now stand at the wood's edge near the council house, where representatives of all five nations will perform the Ritual of Condolence in honor of a recently deceased chief.

PAGE 162 / Translated from the Iroquois by J. N. B. Hewitt (ed. W. Fenton), in *Journal of the Washington Academy of Sciences*, March 15, 1944, p.

75. Like the preceding selection, this too is from the Ritual of Condolence. The orator representing the "elder" nations assuages the grief of the "younger" nations, whom he addresses collectively as "my offspring, you, noble one" (noble because they are chiefs). *Your nephews and nieces*: a stylized way of saying "your fellow clansmen."

PAGE 163 / Translated from the Iroquois by A. C. Parker, in *36th Annual Archaeological Report, being part of Appendix to the Report of the Minister of Education, Ontario, 1928*, p. 14.

PAGE 164 / Translated from the Eskimo by Knud Rasmussen, in his *Intellectual Culture of the Copper Eskimo* (translated from Rasmussen's Danish into English by W. E. Calvert), 1932, p. 53.

PAGES 165-6 / Translated from the Hopi by H. R. Voth, in *Field Museum of Natural History Anthropological Publications*, Vol. 6, No. 1, 1903, pp. 39, 26.

PAGE 167 / Translated from the Papago by Ruth Underhill, in her *Singing for Power*, 1938, p. 140.

PAGE 168 / Translated from the Aztec by Miguel León-Portilla, in his *Pre-Columbian Literatures of Mexico* (copyright 1969 by the University of Oklahoma Press), p. 89.

PAGES 169-70 / Translated from the Sioux by Benjamin Black Elk (son of Black Elk) and revised by John G. Neihardt, in Neihardt's *Black Elk Speaks*, 1932, pp. 170, 262. In the first of these two songs the singer envisions a glorious return to power after humiliating defeats be the whites. The second is sung by Sioux warriors as they attack white troops.

PAGE 171 / Translated from the Cheyenne by James Mooney, in his "The Ghost Dance Religion," *Bureau of American Ethnology, 14th Annual Report, 1892-93*, Part 2, p. 1035. According to Mooney, the crow is here considered lord of the new spirit world. See note to pp. 172-4 below.

PAGES 172-4 / Translated from the Paiute, and from the Comanche, by James Mooney, in his "The Ghost Dance Religion," *Bureau of American Ethnology, 14th Annual Report, 1892-93*, Part 2, pp. 1054-5, 1046-7. The Ghost Dance religion originated in the late nineteenth century among the Paiutes and spread rapidly from tribe to tribe. According to its teaching, the present white-dominated earth was to be replaced by a new world in which Indians would rule unchallenged and all the dead would return to life. For the Plains tribes it promised the return of the vanished buffalo as well. Sometimes the new earth was spoken of as blanketed in snow, and for many it was symbolized by the whirlwind. In the first song on p. 172 the Paiute singer invokes the power of the wind, and in the third song he actually envisions the new snowy earth gliding forth out of the whirling winds.

# Glossary of Tribes, Cultures, and Languages

ACOMA (AK-o-ma). A Pueblo people of New Mexico.

ALGONKIAN. A great language family of eastern North America, including Chippewa, Delaware, Fox, and many others.

APACHE. A native people of New Mexico and Arizona. Related to the Navajo.

ARAPAHO. A buffalo-hunting Plains tribe formerly of eastern Colorado. Survivors are in Oklahoma and Wyoming.

ARAUCANIAN. A group of Indian peoples of central Chile.

AZTEC. A Nahuatl-speaking people of ancient Mexico. Rulers of a vast empire and builders of the pre-conquest city of Mexico (site of present-day Mexico City).

CAKCHIQUEL (COCK-chee-kel). A Mayan people of Guatemala. Closely related to the Quiché.

CHEROKEE. A native people of the Southeastern United States, now divided between North Carolina and Oklahoma.

CHEYENNE. A western Plains tribe, now confined to a reservation in southern Montana.

CHIPPEWA. An Algonkian people of the western Great Lakes region.

COMANCHE. A buffalo-hunting tribe of the southern Great Plains. Survivors are in Oklahoma.

CREEK. A group of native peoples of Georgia and Alabama, now removed to Oklahoma.

CROW. A northern Plains tribe, now mainly confined to a reservation in southern Montana.

DELAWARE. An Algonkian tribe formerly of New Jersey. Survivors are in Oklahoma.

ESKIMO. General name for the natives of the Arctic coasts. All the native peoples of the New World may be termed "Indians" (itself a misnomer, derived from the mistaken belief of Columbus that he had reached a part of Asia) except for the Eskimos, whose distinctive cultural and physical characteristics put them in a class by themselves.

FOX. An Algonkian tribe formerly of Wisconsin. Survivors are in Nebraska.

HOPI. A Pueblo people of northeastern Arizona.

INCA. The pre-conquest culture of Peru. In its narrowest sense, the title of the emperor.

IROQUOIS. Collective name for the Mohawk, Oneida, Onondaga, Cayuga, and Seneca nations of New York and adjacent Canada.

KIOWA (KY-o-way). A southern Plains tribe with survivors in Oklahoma.

KWAKIUTL (kwah-kyoodle). A native people of the coasts of British Columbia.

MAKAH. The native people of Cape Flattery, Washington. Related culturally to the Kwakiutl.

MANDAN. A Sioux-related tribe of North Dakota.

MAYA. A native people of Yucatán. (Maya, in its broadest sense, also includes the Quiché and Cakchiquel of Guatemala.)

NAHUATL (NAH-wattle). Language of the ancient Aztecs, still widely spoken in central Mexico. In this book I use the term Nahuatl (rather than Aztec) to designate material collected in recent times.

NAVAJO (NAHV-a-ho). Largest Indian tribe in the United States today, numbering well over a hundred thousand persons living mainly in northeastern Arizona and adjacent New Mexico. (The spelling "Navaho," with an "h," was introduced in the late nineteenth century, evidently under the assumption that this native people, whose homeland had been appropriated by the United States during the Mexican War, now belonged with *us* and therefore deserved an anglicized name; the Navajo themselves have continued to use the Spanish "j.")

NEZ PERCÉ (nez-purse). An Idaho tribe.

OSAGE. A Sioux-related people formerly of Missouri, now on reservation lands in Oklahoma.

OTOMÍ (oh-doe-MEE). A language of central Mexico, spoken by some hundred thousand people.

PAIUTE (PIE-yoot). A native people of Utah, Nevada, and eastern California.

PAPAGO. A people of southern Arizona. Related to the Pima.

PAWNEE. A once-powerful tribe of the Platte River, now greatly reduced. Survivors are in Oklahoma.

PIMA (PEE-ma). A people of southern Arizona.

PONCA. A Sioux-related tribe living along the Missouri River in northeastern Nebraska.

PUEBLO. A general name for town-dwelling Indians of New Mexico and Arizona. Includes Zuñi, Acoma, the Hopi towns, and many others. ("Pueblo" is the Spanish word for town.)

QUECHUA (KETCH-wa). Language of the ancient Incas, spoken today by several million Indians of Peru. In this book I use the term Quechua (rather than Inca) to designate material collected in recent times.

QUICHÉ (kee-chay). A Mayan people of Guatemala.

SIOUX. General name for a group of related tribes of the northern Mississippi Valley, now living on extensive reservations mostly in the Dakotas.

TEWA (TAY-wa). A Pueblo people of northern New Mexico and northeastern Arizona.

TULE (TOO-lay). A native people of Panama.

TUPI (TOO-pee). An aboriginal language of Brazil, especially of the Amazon Basin.

WINNEBAGO. A Sioux-related Wisconsin tribe, now divided between Wisconsin and Nebraska. Culturally akin to the Algonkians.

WINTU. Small tribe of northern California.

YANA. Extinct tribe of northern California.

ZUÑI (ZOON-yee). A Pueblo people of western New Mexico.

# Suggestions for Further Reading

Astrov, Margot, *The Winged Serpent,* 1946. (Paperback edition, 1962, entitled *American Indian Prose and Poetry.*) This anthology includes extracts from tales and personal memoirs.

Hale, Horatio, *The Iroquois Book of Rites,* 1883. (Reprinted 1963, with an introduction by William N. Fenton.) An elegant presentation of Iroquois history, political customs, and lore pertaining to the great League. Includes the text of the Ritual of Condolence.

León-Portilla, Miguel, *Pre-Columbian Literatures of Mexico,* 1969. Survey of the Aztec and Maya literatures, with examples drawn from the works of various translators.

Matthews, Washington, *Navaho Legends,* 1897. (Reprinted 1969.) A Navajo miscellany, containing two items of particular merit: the Story of the Emergence according to Hatali Nez, and Hatali Natloi's prayer to the thunderbird.

Neihardt, John G., *Black Elk Speaks,* 1932. (Paperback edition, 1961.) A Sioux medicine man recalls his young manhood during the late nineteenth century, the disastrous military campaigns, and the life-restoring visions he believed would save his people. Interspersed with songs and prayers.

Radin, Paul, *The Road of Life and Death: A Ritual Drama of the American Indians,* 1945. The Winnebago Medicine Rite. A long, rather mesmerizing ritual, impressive in its cumulative effect.

Recinos, A., Goetz, Delia, and Morley, Sylvanus G., *Popol Vuh: The Sacred Book of the Ancient Quiché Maya,* 1950. The creation of the world, deeds of mythical heroes, and the migrations of legendary ancestors. Widely regarded as the premier specimen of American Indian literature.

Underhill, Ruth, *Singing for Power: The Song Magic of the Papago Indians of Southern Arizona,* 1938. (Reprinted 1969.) Numerous brief song-texts, presented with a running commentary of unusual interest.